FURNITURE & CABINETMAKING PROJECTS

The best from **FURNITURE** & **CABINETMAKING** magazine

FURNITURE & CABINETMAKING PROJECTS

The best from **FURNITURE** & **CABINETMAKING** magazine

GUILD OF MASTER CRAFTSMAN PUBLICATIONS LTD

This collection first published 1998
by Guild of Master Craftsman Publications Ltd,
Castle Place, 166 High Street, Lewes, East Sussex BN7 1XU

© GMC Publications 1998

ISBN 1 86108 090 5

Printed and bound by Kyodo Printing (Singapore) under the supervision of
MRM Graphics, Winslow, Buckinghamshire, UK

Front cover photograph supplied by Andrew Lawton
Back cover photograph supplied by Kevin Ley

CONTENTS

NOTES

PLEASE note that names, addresses, prices etc were correct at the time the articles were originally published, but may since have changed.

MEASUREMENTS

THROUGHOUT the book instances will be found where a metric measurement has fractionally varying imperial equivalents, usually within $\frac{1}{16}$in either way. This is because in each particular case the closest imperial equivalent has been given. A mixture of metric and imperial measurements should NEVER be used – always use either one or the other.

INTRODUCTION

SINCE the eighteenth century, when cabinetmakers such as Chippendale, Sheraton and Hepplewhite produced their 'Directors', or pattern books, furniture-makers have extensively used such material to research both design and construction.

With the virtual demise of craft education and apprenticeships in recent times the written word has become even more important – for many, it is their only link with other makers, and the only source from which to learn.

So, ideally, a furniture project is far more than a pattern to be followed. It should be an opportunity to look over the shoulder of the maker, to see not only what is done, but how and why – crossbanding is thus revealed as both a decorative device and a practical method of preventing veneered surfaces from splintering at their edges.

Details of equipment and materials used should mesh neatly with aesthetic considerations, showing how the nuts and bolts of cabinetmaking go to make up the finished piece.

The projects in this book, compiled from *Furniture & Cabinetmaking* magazine, have been selected because they provide just this blend of inspiration, problem-solving and information. A huge range of types, styles and periods is represented, but all are by experienced craftsmen with years of hard-won expertise to share.

Whether making one of the pieces shown, or using the approaches and techniques revealed to make something quite different, these pages will prove their worth time and again in producing well-designed, soundly made and practical furniture.

Paul Richardson,
Editor, *Furniture & Cabinetmaking* magazine

Refined by design

David Charlesworth on the importance of reference for the furniture designer and maker

NOT MANY CASUAL observers, admiring a finished piece of furniture, appreciate the hours of thought, the multitude of decisions and the care that go into the design before a single cut is made. I would like to try and demonstrate this here by explaining the design and making of a circular oak (*Quercus robur*) dining table with curved laminate legs.

Personally I do not subscribe to the dogma of original design. The self-conscious striving after this is all too well illustrated in some student work where the results are often ugly, attention seeking and impractical. Furniture has been made for more than 2000 years and new ideas are as rare as hen's teeth.

This commission followed one where I had been asked to copy some Edward Barnsley chairs. A carver and a side chair were produced to complete a set of six which had been split. Next the client; who is a keen collector of Barnsley's work, required a circular dining table to seat six.

As I had worked on these exact copies, a sense of frustration had begun to creep in. They were beautiful chairs and very challenging to make, but the desire to change certain details had become stronger and stronger. I had resisted the temptation, but was now in the mood to try an original design.

I started by considering a Barnsley design from 1975, pictured in the catalogue for a major retrospective exhibition of his work held in 1982.

This table had a pedestal with a laminated curved element and a rather straight foot. The foot in particular bothered me. It was reminiscent of so much of the design of that time, and seemed out of place next to the graceful curved lamination.

Betty's table

Then I remembered an elegant yew table which Ted Baly had made during my training year in his workshop near Dartington almost 20 years before. I arranged to visit his wife Betty, as I knew that she still had this particular table.

On my return I consulted the workshop's extensive library of books and magazines. In Alan Peter's book *Cabinetmaking the Professional Approach*, there was a table which excited me. The generous feet and asymmetric curves have an Oriental feel and all the curved elements are, in fact, cut from solid. The top of the leg curve is achieved by shaping the end grain of the top rail.

With these three designs in mind I started to sketch and soon came up with a variation in the form of a stretched C.

Can it be done?

The four C-shaped legs would need to be joined at their centres; I decided to mitre-joint them as Ted had done. Whereas he had used dowels to locate and reinforce the joint, I would use large biscuits on account of their superior glue surface area.

This is not as difficult as it sounds, although it does call for some special clamping blocks to be carefully designed and made. There is an all-embracing rule which states "clamping force should be perpendicular to the glue surface and pass through the centre of the surface." This is one of the most useful guides to assembly and, if used correctly, glue ups, which are nerve-wracking at the best of times, will go much more smoothly.

When a section of the joint was drawn it became apparent that the width of leg required would need to be relatively large. Here was the crux of the problem. A laminated leg was the obvious solution, but all the sketches called for a gently tapering width – delicate at the top, massive at the centre of the joint and intermediate for a substantial foot.

Solution

The library was consulted again and the answer appeared in *Tage Frid Teaches Woodworking, volume two, pages 10 to 26*. Here was a method

PICTURE BY TIM MACAIRE

"This project is only suitable for a serious masochist or the totally deranged"

of producing tapered laminates with a simple jig in the thicknesser. This was exciting, as I had never consciously seen this technique used in any other piece of furniture, and it would produce the exact shape that had been sketched.

There was also another invaluable idea in this section of the book. His home-made clamping system based on studding and hexagonal bar would replace a calculated requirement for more than £500 worth of heavy G clamps, most of which I did not possess.

This is a brilliant solution, the entire clamping set-up costing about £25 in materials and about half a day's work in a friend's engineering workshop. The other advantage of this system is that many clamping points can be spaced close together along the 'circumference' of the curve to produce the enormous pressure that is required for minimal glue lines.

There is a salutory section on this topic in Bruce Hoadly's *Understanding Wood*, which I would recommend to all serious cabinet-makers. Studding used for clamping produces a very light solution as the threaded bar is in tension.

Page 24 of Robert Wearing's *The Resourceful Woodworker* also shows ingenious methods for carcass clamping using studding and curved bearers. Compare the cost and weight of this method with the use of sash cramps.

As a result of all this research I was now reasonably confident that my design was feasible – and it was time to begin.

Tapered lamination

It was difficult to find three inch oak of sufficient width and straightness from which to cut the laminates. However, there was some suitable stuff left over from a balcony job some 15 years before.

The laminates were bandsawn using a point fence with my favourite stainless 'meat and fish' blade which has a kerf of only 1.5mm. Initially, 15 4.8mm pieces were required per leg. Incidentally, the Editor has conceived this as a project article, but my advice is that it would only be suitable for a serious masochist or the totally deranged – I include myself in both categories!

The 'inlays' in the legs are in fact laminates of solid sycamore (*Acer pseudoplatanus*) so 13 slices of oak and one of sycamore were used – but it is advisable to cut several spares in case the thicknesser eats some. The sequence is to machine plane the edge of the stock, bandsaw a slice, then re-machine the sawn edge, removing the minimum to clean off the saw marks, about 0.2mm in this case. The length of stuff had been pre-cut to fit the stops on the tapering jig.

Tapering jig

I started with a thicknessed length of stable stuff. The undulating top surface was then marked out with great care on both edges, using measurements calculated from a full-size drawing of one leg.

A centre line was drawn and radial width measurements were taken at regular intervals along this line, *see*

fig 1. These were than divided by 15 to give the thickness of the laminate at each interval. The same intervals were marked along the length of the jig and the relevant thickness gauged down from the top surface at every interval. These points were then joined into a far curved line, *see fig 2*, which was bandsawn close, *see fig 3*, and then planed, spokeshaved and scraped.

Accuracy in thickness across the width is very important here. When stacking 15 layers an error of 0.1mm in each layer will produce an error of 1.5mm in the result.

End stops were glued to the jig. These help to reduce the shock as it approaches the cutter block in the thicknesser, *see fig 4*, as the leading end is secured under the outfeed roller before the cutting of the laminate begins.

You will see from the drawing that our 4.8mm piece is being planed ➤

LEFT: David Charlesworth's table with curved, tapered, laminated legs.

ABOVE: Alan Peters' table from his book, Cabinetmaking, the Professional Approach.

BELOW: The Edward Baly table.

MAKING THE TAPERED LAMINATES

FIGURE 1

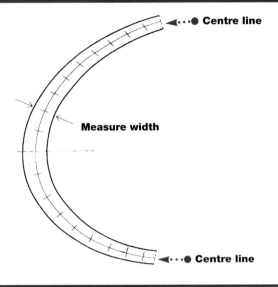

Centre line

Measure width

Centre line

Draw the leg at full size, then mark a centre line. Use compasses to mark and number uniform intervals (say, 75mm) from centre zero along the centre line

Measure the width of the leg at each interval, giving W0, W1, W2 etc. Divide each measurement by the number of laminates (15 in this instance).

FIGURE 2

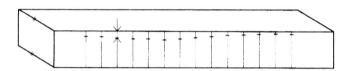

On a piece of timber suitable for the thicknesser jig, mark and number the same intervals along both edges. At each interval gauge down from the top 'W' minus 2mm divided by 15 on both edges. Join these points to form a fair curve.

FIGURE 3

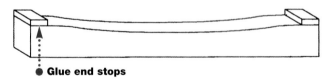

Glue end stops

Remove the waste from above this line to form a curved bed, and fix end-stops.

FIGURE 4

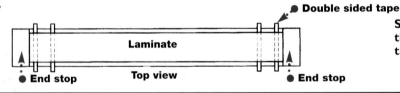

Double sided tape

Laminate

End stop   Top view   End stop

Secure the first laminate to the jig using double-sided tape.

FIGURE 5

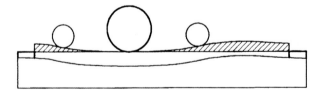

Pass the assembly through the thicknesser. Wear eye protection and stand well clear when thicknessing very thin stock in this way. The feed rollers push the laminate down into the curve and cut the top surface flat, producing this evenly tapered shape.

FIGURE 6

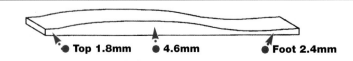

Top 1.8mm   4.6mm   Foot 2.4mm

"Stand well clear when attempting to produce such thin stuff in the thicknesser"

down to 1.8mm at its thin end, *fig 5*. This requires extremely sharp blades and it also helps to secure the end of the laminate, *see fig 6*, with two narrow cross pieces of double-sided Sellotape, one at the end and one about three inches in. These prevent the laminate from being picked up, eaten and spat out in bits. Always wear eye protection and stand well clear when attempting to produce such thin stuff in the thicknesser. I believe it can only be done by fixing the work to something more substantial with double-sided tape or glue.

When the first few trial laminates were produced they seemed to be slightly thicker in the centre than at the edges. Perhaps these edges were bouncing a little under the pounding of the blades? I decided to damp the top surface just before thicknessing. This induced a downward curve across the width and the result was edges slightly thicker than the centre – exactly what was required for tight glue lines.

Template sanding

I like to draw complex components such as this leg full-size on melamine-faced hardboard. A template and the bending former to finished size was marked out adjacent to the inner surface of the leg. The horizontal centre line and the vertical reference line are essential.

Templates for this operation need to be about 10mm undersize so both pieces can be produced from one sheet of hardboard, *see fig 7*.

The bending former

Shuttering ply was stacked to form this with better quality ply top and bottom. After gluing, the underside and top were planed flat to act as reference surfaces. The shape was marked and bandsawn with the aid of the template which was fixed temporarily to the underside.

A sanding disc set-up was then employed to smooth the edge of the former and bring it to finished size. Many years ago I had performed this operation with spokeshaves and ➤

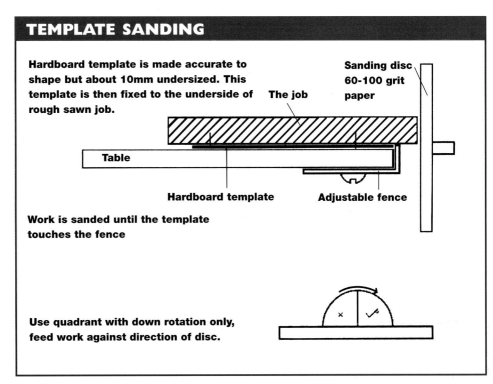

TEMPLATE SANDING

Hardboard template is made accurate to shape but about 10mm undersized. This template is then fixed to the underside of rough sawn job.

Sanding disc 60-100 grit paper

The job

Table

Hardboard template

Adjustable fence

Work is sanded until the template touches the fence

Use quadrant with down rotation only, feed work against direction of disc.

FIGURE 7

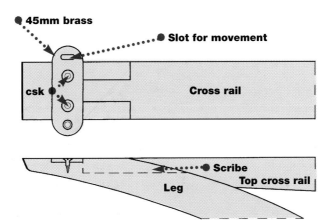

45mm brass

Slot for movement

csk

Cross rail

Scribe

Leg

Top cross rail

Detail of fixings & top cross rail to leg joint

LEFT: Race against time – clamping the laminates using the Tage Frid method.

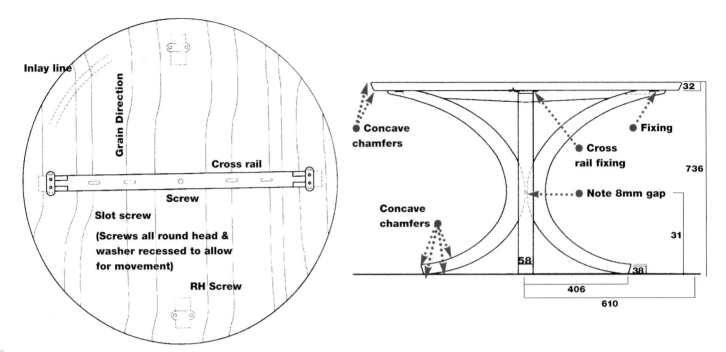

Inlay line

Grain Direction

Cross rail

Screw

Slot screw

(Screws all round head & washer recessed to allow for movement)

RH Screw

● **Concave chamfers**

● **Fixing**

● **Cross rail fixing**

● **Note 8mm gap**

Concave chamfers

32

736

31

58   38

406

610

"A router cutter was used with a one penny piece fixed off centre to act as a fence"

● The books referred to in this article are:

● Cabinet Making – the Professional Approach. by Alan Peters, published in 1984 by Stobart Davies, ISBN 085442 024X

● Tage Frid Teaches Woodworking, published in 1981 by Taunton Press, ISBN 0-918804-11-6

● Understanding Wood, by Bruce Hoadly, published in 1981 by Taunton Press, ISBN 0-918804-05-1

● The Resourceful Woodworker, Tools Techniques & Tricks of the Trade by Bob Wearing, published in 1991 by Batsford, ISBN 07134 6485 2

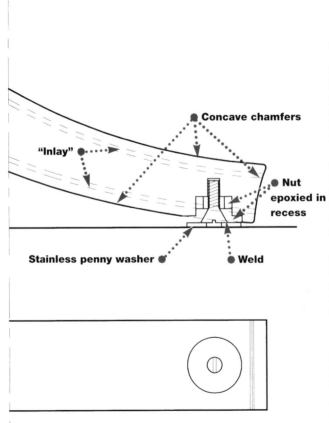

"Inlay"

● **Concave chamfers**

● **Nut epoxied in recess**

Stainless penny washer ●   ● **Weld**

FIGURE 8   **Underside view**

circular plane but it wasn't much fun.

Holes were then drilled for the Frid clamping system and the whole lined with builders' polythene. Waxed pegs were also fitted to prevent lateral and longitudinal slip, the stack of laminates being notched in the centre to engage the centre line pegs.

Bob Seymour from Millthorne chairs helped with the glue-up as time was limited to the 15 minutes allowed by Aerolite glue. We found that we only had the strength to bend eight laminates at a time, so each leg had to be glued in two sessions.

A heavy duty ratchet hold-down strap was used to hold the initial bend while we added the crosspieces and tightened the nuts, working from the centre outwards. Our record was about 12 minutes.

Mitres and biscuits

After cleaning up the edges of the legs they were returned to the former for the feet, tops and mitre joints to be marked out relative to the template, and its centre and vertical lines. The final hand planing of the mitres and biscuit joint cutting were both achieved with the aid of simple jigs clamped to the surface.

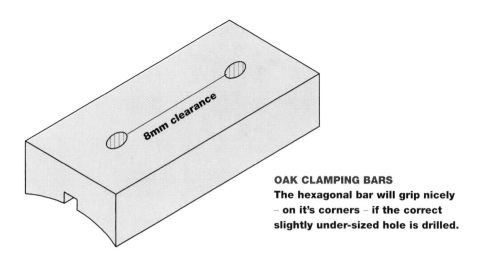

OAK CLAMPING BARS
**The hexagonal bar will grip nicely
– on it's corners – if the correct
slightly under-sized hole is drilled.**

● From a
converted barn at
his Harton Manor,
North Devon
home, DAVID
CHARLESWORTH
runs private
courses on the
making of fine
furniture. He
trained with
Edward Baly,
principal founder
member of the
Devon Guild of
Craftsmen, and
turned to
teaching from
making
commissioned
pieces for clients.
He can be reached
on 01237 441288.

**LEFT: Preparation for jointing
the laminated elements.**

Dry glue up

Special clamping blocks were made
to ensure that clamping pressure was
directed through the centre of the
relatively small glue surface. Pairs of
legs were offered up to check the fit
of inner curved surfaces and the
white 'inlay' lines.

After adjustments had been made,
pairs were glued together. The final
pair of mitred surfaces was now
flattened and glued. The small
square hole left at the centre of this
four way joint was deliberate,
see drawing of table plan, as I
wanted to avoid a dust trap at this
vase-shaped intersection. Special
tools had to be made to remove
surplus glue from this area at the
final assembly.

Concave mouldings

These are much used in antique
Chinese work and they gather and
reflect light in a pleasing manner. I
wanted this concave chamfer to
change its width along the length of
the leg in the same way that the
'inlay' width varied with the
changing leg sections.

A router cutter was used with a
one penny piece fixed off centre

below the cutter to act as a fence.
If the router is held facing in a
particular direction for the entire cut,
the varying width of chamfer can be
achieved, if you see what I mean.

The rest of the construction was
relatively straightforward. Fixing
plates for the top were produced
from 5mm brass, one pair
with slots to allow for the seasonal
movement of the solid timber,
see fig 7.

Adjustable stainless levellers were
made for the feet as floors are rarely
flat and I wanted to avoid the
possibility of wear at the base of the
toes, *see fig 8*.

Delivery

The table duly delivered, both
customer and maker were delighted
by the final result. This is not always
the case, so the effort of carrying
the table through the precipitous
and vehicle-less side streets of
Polruan, Cornwall seemed well
worthwhile.

I hope that some of these
techniques will be of interest and can
be incorporated in readers' projects –
I would be interested to hear of any
successful or innovative applications. ■

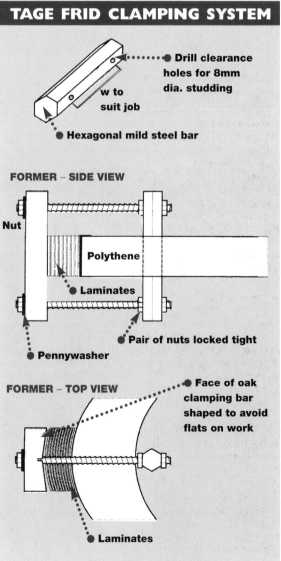

TAGE FRID CLAMPING SYSTEM

● **Drill clearance
holes for 8mm
dia. studding**

w to
suit job

● **Hexagonal mild steel bar**

FORMER – SIDE VIEW

Nut

Polythene

● **Laminates**

● **Pair of nuts locked tight**

● **Pennywasher**

FORMER – TOP VIEW

● **Face of oak
clamping bar
shaped to avoid
flats on work**

● **Laminates**

Speculating in sy

Kevin Ley makes a Shaker-influenced lady's writing desk from a timber which used to be more at home in the kitchen

● On leaving the RAF in 1987 KEVIN LEY set to turning his hobby into a commercial proposition. The former squadron leader designs and makes bespoke furniture from his cottage and workshop in Shropshire.

BELOW: Kevin Ley checks the slide clearance of his lady's writing desk

I N THE PAST sycamore (*Acer pseudoplatanus*) was a utilitarian wood used for draining and wash boards, butchers' blocks and kitchen tables, and other utensils which came into contact with food; the close grain and pale colour allowed surfaces to be left unsealed while bleaching and scrubbing kept everything hygienic and looking good.

The Georgians used figured sycamore as a decorative veneer on fine pieces, although generally stained grey and referred to as 'harewood'.

The first time I saw and touched natural-finished sycamore, however, I was fascinated by the silky texture, gently understated figuring and creamy colour.

Deciding it would lend itself well to delicate work, I designed this lady's writing desk and its chair, *see 'Shaker leg'*, to be made as a speculative piece.

Timber selection

This moderately priced British hardwood is in plentiful supply, but must be felled in winter when the sap is down, and seasoned in an upright position – 'end-reared' – after conversion to boards and before kilning.

This treatment prevents staining from the sap, and penetrating sticker marks. Ideal drying conditions are cold nights and warm sunny days.

When buying, try to obtain a guarantee that the job has been done properly because the sap staining is an ugly, dirty, grey which I have not found any satisfactory method of removing; bleaching seems to turn it an equally ugly green.

Surface staining is of a similar colour, but comes off on the first pass over the planer; so it pays to test the wood with a small plane before buying.

Good sized, clean, through-and-through boards are usually available; quarter-sawn sycamore has an interesting lacy figure which blends in well as a special feature, perhaps for drawer fronts or door panels.

Rarer and more expensive is ripple or fiddleback sycamore, much coveted for musical instruments. I feel that a little of

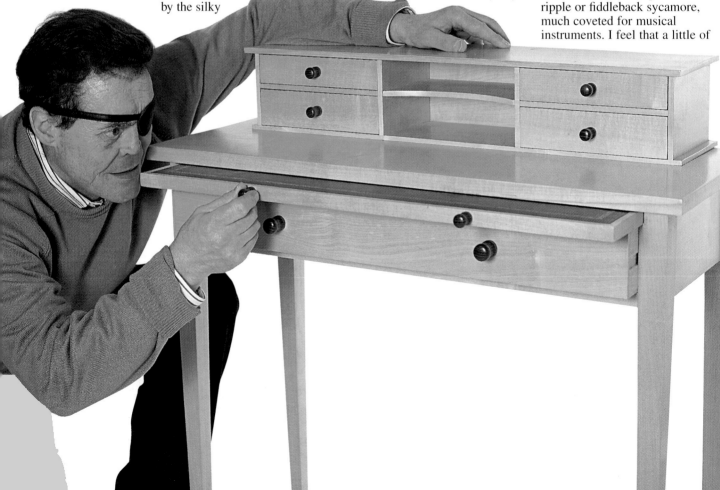

amore

this goes a long way in furniture; it can easily become fussy.

Design

This design is based on the traditional bonheur du jour, or small writing desk, but with a strong Shaker influence.

Space efficiency is good; with the chair placed under the table little room is taken up; the top gives a display area, the drawers good storage, and the slide under the top a decent extra writing surface.

The desk slips easily into most settings in most houses, being particularly useful in small rooms or niches, so making an excellent hall or telephone table.

The pieces pictured here have been displayed at local exhibitions, and design developments have evolved from both.

Table construction

Mortise the legs before tapering, and begin the taper 150mm, 6in down from the top of the leg. The tapers can be achieved with jigs on the planer-thicknesser or circular saw; but I find the simplest, safest, and most enjoyable method is to rough them out on the bandsaw and finish by hand, as the wood is such a joy to plane.

Round over the feet of the legs, see fig 1. Cut the tenons on the front drawer rail, sides, and back.

Before assembly recess the sides and front legs to take the slide. The sides and back should have recesses cut for the expansion brackets to which the top will attach; make sure that those in the sides are set well back to clear the slide.

The position of the brackets should be set just below the level of the top, so that it is pulled

tightly down onto the sides and back when fixed.

Fit the brackets' faces with countersunk holes into these recesses; make them a snug fit as movement need not be allowed for at this point.

Suspension runners

The drawer suspension runners should also be made and fitted

now. To ensure accurate running of the drawers, cut a test slot in a piece of scrap using the router cutter that will later be used to slot the drawer sides. Dimension the runners to fit tightly into this, so that only micro adjustment will be necessary later.

Screw and glue them into place on the sides.

Dry fit all the joints before ➤

BELOW: A light and simple design, with interest added by the contrasting fumed oak pulls and the writing slide

"Make sure the screws don't inadvertently go right through the top!"

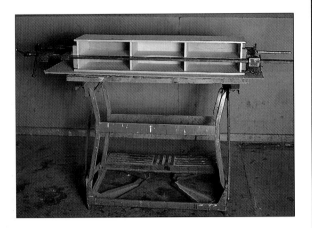

ABOVE: Carefully sequenced clamping of the upper superstructure is necessary

gluing, finishing all the surfaces as far as possible. Glue and clamp the sides to the legs, checking for square, and leave to set. When dry these two sub-assemblies are joined by gluing and clamping the back and the front drawer rail to the legs; again check for square in all directions and leave to set.

Prepare top

Prepare the top for fitting by cutting recesses for the expansion brackets. The bracket's slotted faces are fitted to the top; make sure the screws are placed in the correct slots to allow movement across the grain!

The recesses must be oversize in the direction of movement – front to back and vice versa – to allow for expansion or contraction of the top. Be very careful to ensure that the brackets are set deep enough to allow the slide to move without fouling the brackets or the screw heads.

Cut two slots in the underside of the top to take the slide stop screws, *see next paragraph*; they should stop 75mm, 3in back from the front of the top. Fit the top to the brackets, making sure the screws don't inadvertently go right through the top!

Drawer and slide

The drawer also fulfils the function of lopers in that it supports the slide when extended. To achieve this, fit two fixed dowels to the underside of the slide, projecting downwards and set back 75mm, 3in from the front. These engage the drawer front as the slide is pulled out, causing the drawer to be opened with it, thus providing the necessary support, *see fig 2*.

The drawer is of traditional construction The drawer casings are cedar (*Cedrus libani*), and the bottom 4mm, $^5/_{32}$in cedar-veneered MDF. The sides are slotted to take the runners using the router cutter mentioned above.

The drawer should be fitted carefully; as it takes the weight of the slide, play between the runners and slot should be as small as possible while allowing free movement. Finally cut two

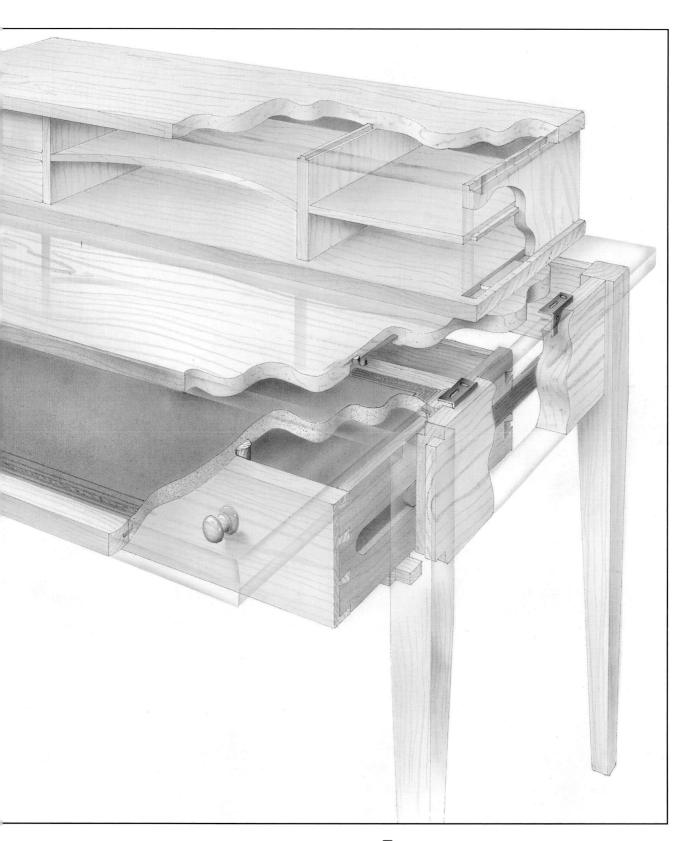

scallops out of the back of the drawer to allow it to be fitted and removed without fouling the slide's dowels.

To prevent the slide being pulled right out, fit two filed-down screws through its back edge; these run in the stopped slots cut earlier in the underside of the top, *see above*.

These are screwed into place after the slide has been positioned and before the drawer is fitted.

Check the slide carefully for clearance; to prevent any scuffing of its skiver when it is in use, the underside of the table top should be covered with a piece of baize.

Top carcass

The top carcass is a straight-forward construction in 10mm, $^3/_8$in thick stock with backs of 4mm, $^5/_{32}$in sycamore-veneered MDF. The drawer unit can be fixed to the top in a number of ways; that shown is by shouldered tenons through the base, let in to mortises in the table top. ➤

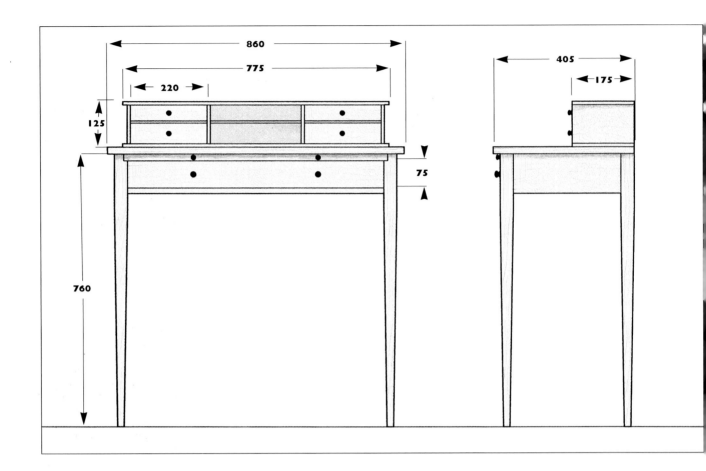

Brackets, dowels or screws could be used on the back edges. One client wanted the option of removing the drawer unit, and did not want the top defaced, so we located it on the top with Blu-Tack to stop it slipping, a technique which I understand is still satisfactory!

Dimension all the pieces and cut mortises in the top and bottom to take the uprights – remembering to make the appropriate through cuts in the base for the shouldered tenons, if required.

Mortise the uprights to take the shelves, and slot them for the backs. Tenon the uprights and shelves, and cut the curved front on the middle shelf.

Dry assemble all the joints to check the fit, and finish all the pieces. Gluing up is a little tricky, and I used the following method, *see photo:* glue the shelves and backs in to the uprights – do not glue the tops or bottoms of the backs – and dry fit the top and bottom; pull up the shelf and back joints with sash cramps back and front; check for square and leave to set.

When dry, carefully remove the top and bottom, apply glue to the joints and re-fit them. Clamp them up, check for square and leave to set.

Make and fit the drawers – again the casings are cedar and the bottoms cedar-veneered MDF, glued in all round.

Contrasting detail

To provide extra detail interest to the piece I use a contrasting timber such as rosewood (*Dalbergia sp*), or in this case fumed oak (*Quercus robur*), for the knobs. Turn and finish the pieces on the lathe, using a sizing tool to make the spigots, oil and fit.

Finishing

Check all the joints for glue squeeze-out, then clean up ready for the finish. I apply three coats of an acrylic water-based varnish – preferably one with a UV filter incorporated to minimise yellowing or darkening – to the sycamore; rub down to denib between coats.

Fit the knobs and the leather skiver; and finish with two coats of clear wax, buffing to a gentle sheen.

Conclusion

The small mechanical element made this an interesting piece to build, and one that has enjoyed success in several directions. I still have the prototype in my house – and it continues to generate work.

● See 'Shaker Leg', on facing page, for details of the accompanying chair.

Shaker leg

The perfect companion to a lady's writing desk, this Shaker-influenced chair was made by **Kevin Ley** to complete the set

"Harewood was derived from 'air-wood', being as light as air"

LEFT: A pleasant, Shaker-influenced chair in sycamore with fumed oak finials

THIS IS VERY much a Shaker design, the tapers on the legs and rails and the thin seat-frame keeping it light and dainty. Sycamore is especially appropriate; its Georgian name 'harewood' was derived from 'air-wood', being as light as air.

The light construction does, however, require great accuracy and care in the jointing to ensure that it can withstand the severe stresses placed on a chair – even one to be used by a lady!

Plans

First make a set of full-size drawings – plan and elevations – on a piece of hardboard or similar, from which the angles of the joints and precise dimensions may be taken.

Cut the legs to size, cut all the mortises, and drill the 13mm,

ABOVE RIGHT: The chair with its companion writing table

"Gluing the seat in would be disastrous if it were made from solid wood, as shrinkage would cause splitting almost immediately"

$\frac{1}{2}$in holes for the stretchers. The top of the back legs can be drilled for the finials at this stage.

Taper the front legs, and 150mm, 6in each end of the back legs. I hand plane these after roughing out on the bandsaw as sycamore is so workable, but a tapering jig can be made for most static machines if preferred. Slot the inside corners of the legs to accept the seat, *see illustration*; then radius the tops and bottoms – except the top inside edges of the mortised faces – of the front legs.

Make the seat frame-rails, cutting the tenons at the angle required for the front to back taper of the seat. This angle can be measured from the full-size ▶

LEFT: **Fumed oak finials are spigoted into holes in the back legs**

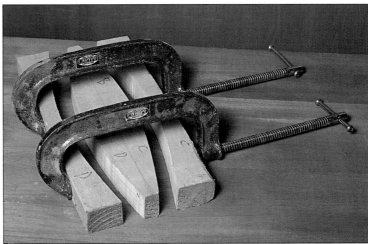

ABOVE: **A simple former for producing the steam-bent back rails**

"The fumed oak finials are turned with spigots to fit the holes in the top of the back legs"

plan drawing. Cut the stretchers to length from 19 by 19mm, $^3/_4$ by $^3/_4$ in stock. The taper on these runs from 19mm, $^3/_4$ in at the centre to 13mm, $^1/_2$ in at the ends; I use a sizing tool on the lathe to ensure the ends are a consistent good fit. If no lathe is available these components can be shaped using a spokeshave, but pay careful attention to the diameter of the ends where they are jointed into the legs.

Curved rails

From 8mm, $^5/_{16}$ in stock cut four back rails – one spare just in case! – work the tenons' shoulders and cut the top curve while these parts are flat. Steam for about 30 minutes before clamping to a former, *see photo*, giving about 19mm, $^3/_4$ in of

curvature at the centre.

Leave overnight to set; then angle and finish the tenons with a small hand plane to fit the 6mm, $^1/_4$ in mortises in the back legs.

Dry fit all the joints, make any necessary adjustments and then finish all the individual components; glue, assemble and clamp the back and front sub-assemblies. Check for square and leave to set.

Cut the seat to size from 6mm sycamore-veneered ply or MDF; cut out the leg rebates in its corners.

Assembly

Finish assembling the chair by gluing and clamping the side seat rails and stretchers to the back and front; with the seat glued into its slot all round. Once

again check for square and leave to set.

Gluing the seat in would be disastrous if it were made from solid wood, as shrinkage would cause splitting almost immediately. As ours is made of stable veneered material, though, it will strengthen the structure and remove the need for corner braces.

The fumed oak finials are turned with spigots to fit the holes in the top of the back legs, and are glued in place.

The seat can be used as it is or with a loose or tie-on cushion. ▨

■ **See previous article, 'Speculating in sycamore', for details of the accompanying writing desk**

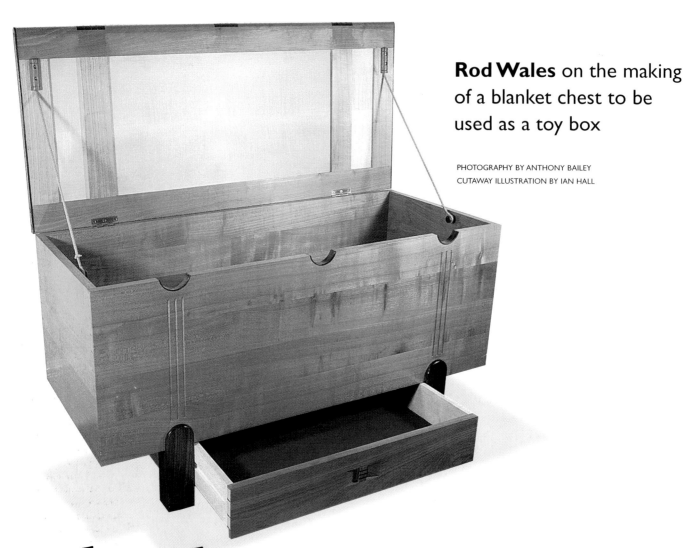

Rod Wales on the making of a blanket chest to be used as a toy box

PHOTOGRAPHY BY ANTHONY BAILEY
CUTAWAY ILLUSTRATION BY IAN HALL

Blanket coverage

ABOVE: A blanket chest that can function as a toy box

ABOVE: Bridle jointed feet form part of the drawer and rail assembly

THIS PIECE WAS commissioned for a generously proportioned entrance hall. Its overall dimensions were specified, as was the requirement for a drawer.

The various elements of the construction are integrated without allowing the visual unity to overwhelm, so becoming homogeneous and bland. Thus, details are echoed – but intentionally not repeated – to give the chest a degree of harmonious complexity.

The carcass, lid frame and drawer front are in English cherry (*Prunus avium*), the lid panels in sycamore (*Acer pseudoplatanus*), and the feet, handles and details in African padauk (*Pterocarpus soyauxii*).

Carcass

First the cherry is planked up, prepared to size and the edges shot by hand, biscuited and assembled.

The use of lap dovetails ensures the front elevation is visually uninterrupted. They are spaced symmetrically from the centre, the joints in pairs, decreasing in width towards the edges of the panel, so producing a visual tension.

The lap is 6mm, $^1/_4$in on a 22mm, $^7/_8$in panel thickness. After marking out and sawing, the majority of the waste is removed from the tail sockets with a router.

Once the pins are cut and pared on the front and back panels, the tails are marked out from these with the pin panels temporarily supported.

The bottom dovetail accommodates a 6mm, $^1/_4$in groove to take the bottom panel; this is 10mm, $^3/_8$in thick MDF rebated to form a 6mm, $^1/_4$in tongue.

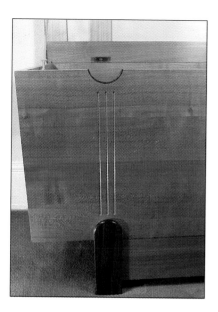

LEFT: Feet, fluting and handles must line up

JOINT OPTION

FACED WITH TWO jointing options for the carcass – a tongued mitre (or biscuit) or dovetailing – I decided on the latter, despite the extra time involved.

Indeed, since this piece was made a number of dovetail jigs have appeared on the market which would accomplish this scale of dovetailing very well indeed.

It would be foolish, however, to make the not inconsiderable investment in such a jig without a continuous need for it.

A mitre joint could have been cut in a tenth of the time by a panel saw, but I felt the side of the chest needed some incident to offset the concentration of detail on the front. Moreover, dovetails are more traditional on a chest, which is one of the earliest furniture types, and add a feeling of robustness.

● **ROD WALES** works with his partner Alison at their Chiddingly, Sussex workshop. Alison studied for a degree in fine art before going on to Rycotewood for a year and then working for John Makepeace; meanwhile Rod had gone on to Parnham from Rycotewood. They set up their workshop in 1981 and largely spend their time designing for themselves and for others, making models and prototypes and marketing their pieces.

LEFT: Lid handle is a split turning, the lid's leading edge is bullnosed to it

Joints for feet

Before clean-up and assembly the long- and short-shouldered bridle joints for the feet must be cut. The long front side is shaped to a semi-circle at the top, and the short shoulder on the inside butts up to the underside of the bottom panel.

I used a ply template, and a template follower on the router, to cut the recess on the outside of the panel.

The semi-circle in the template can be cut with a tank cutter or expansion bit.

The tangential lines on the front of the panel are squared up from the bottom edge to each end of the semi-circle, sawn and pared back. The short recess on the inside of the carcass panels can be simply routed and pared.

For accuracy, cramp together

"I might be accused of using belt and braces here, but then again my trousers don't often fall down"

the front and the back panels and square across the positions of the bridle joints on the bottom edges to line up the template, which will be slightly wider than the joint itself.

After preparing the feet to exact length, width and thickness, the bridle joint can be cut in these. Use a template for the shape of the feet to ensure accuracy; this can be test-fitted into the recess.

Although the foot could be shaped with a router following

the template, I chose to do this with a disc sander. Routing would have been against the grain in places, and sanding to remove burn marks and tear-out would spoil the fit into the recess.

After fitting, the face is given a 3mm, $^1/_8$in chamfer, which is also taken round the bottom edges of the foot.

Handles and recesses

The handle recesses are sawn into the top of the front panel, ➤

"I couldn't accurately predict how much the decorative-thickness veneers would compress"

then routed from a template, the same template being used to make the negative side of a laminating former for the handles themselves.

The radius for the positive side of this former is theoretically that of the negative less the thickness of the lay up. However, as I couldn't accurately predict how much the decorative-thickness veneers would compress, I used a slightly smaller radius and lined the former with thick cork to take up any tolerance.

The veneer strips are cut with a generous allowance in the width, and the former itself is thicker than the chest panel. The final lay up should be 5mm, $^{13}/_{64}$ in thick.

After completing the laminates,

the surface of the veneer to be fixed to the edge of the chest is lightly sanded before gluing with an epoxy cement.

Since much of the gluing surface is end-grain, the laminate is also pinned at either end, the heads punched in, then one last veneer laminated on to hide the fixing. I might be accused of using belt and braces here, but then again my trousers don't often fall down!

Fluting detail

With the handles in place and trimmed, the fluting on the front panel can be marked out centrally to handle and foot, then routed in.

Check the depth on scrap

material and rout against a batten cramped to the panel. Be careful not to linger at the beginning and end of the cuts as the consequent burning is awkward to remove without destroying the crispness of the line.

If any problems do occur with this, grind a scraper to the profile of the flute and make a special sanding block, but be careful not to round over or enlarge the edges of the flutes.

The carcass is now ready for preliminary sanding and assembly.

Drawer and frame

The drawer frame consists of two side rails tenoned into the middle of the feet; the back rail is stub

THIS PROJECT featured in greater detail in Rod Wales' Furniture Projects book, published by Guild of Master Craftsman Publications, ISBN 0 946819 25 4, and available by post from their head office at Castle Place, 166 High Street, Lewes, East Sussex BN7 1XU.

This book, published in 1991 and reprinted in 1993, contains 15 projects for domestic and office furniture, with cutting lists, and incorporates advice on problem-solving and the author's notes on the design processes involved.

LEFT: Recessed, dovetail section handle

tenoned and positioned symmetrically to the drawer front, 1mm, $^5/_{64}$in inside the carcass plane; the drawer rail is also stub tenoned.

Due to the position of the side rails a drawer guide was necessary; this also serves as a mount for the drawer runner, It is housed into the side rail and stub tenoned front and back; the tenon counteracts the weight of the side-hung drawer. After fitting, the guide is housed to take the runner.

The shoulder lengths of the side, back and drawer rails are critical, there being little or no tolerance if the feet are firmly joined to the carcass. These dimensions are best checked off the feet themselves, knocked home dry into the carcass.

The drawer rail between the two front feet is set back to allow the drawer front to oversail. The runner need only be screwed into its housing, lest subsequent easing be required when fitting the drawer.

Underframe assembly

Assembly of the underframe includes the fitting of the feet, so requires two pairs of hands and a glue with an open-assembly time of at least 20 minutes.

Once the glue is applied, knock home the rails into the feet, cramp the feet down onto the carcass to bring the bridle joint home; cramp the rails.

When cleaning up squeeze-out, be particularly rigorous around the projecting curved bridle joint.

Drawer

As the single drawer is side-hung, a false front is unnecessary. The drawer is entirely standard-issue with lap dovetails at the front, through dovetails at the back, and the bottom is grooved in under the back.

The sides and back are of sycamore to match the lid panels; the bottom of 6mm, $^1/_4$in ply is rebated into the grooves.

The component parts are first fitted to the opening; the tail sockets are cut fractionally shallow in the front and back. ➤

Front elevation

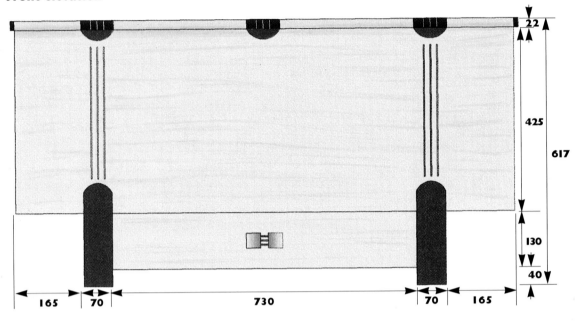

22
425
617
130
40
165 | 70 | 730 | 70 | 165

Plan

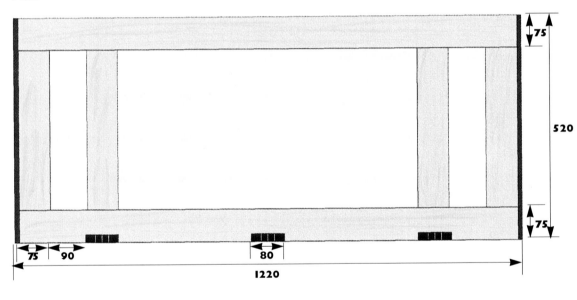

75
520
75
75 | 90 | 80
1220

When assembled, the sides are thus slightly proud, and can then be planed back to the end of the pins.

With the runners removed, the assembled drawer can be fitted to the opening, and the position of the groove to take the runner measured and routed. This groove need only be a maximum of 6mm, $^{1}/_{4}$in deep, but necessitates a slightly thicker drawer side than usual.

The pull is best marked out and cut prior to gluing up the drawer. The central recess is routed and the sloping sides pared down to it. The dovetail-section insert – inlaid with padauk – is glued in.

As the inlays in the handle are left proud, a cork-faced block is advisable when cramping.

Making lid

The traditionally-constructed lid employs haunched mortises and tenons for the end rails, the stub tenoned internal rails lining up with the feet and fluting on the carcass. Solid sycamore panels are rebated into grooves in the framework, and are set 1mm, $^{3}/_{64}$in down from the top face.

After routing this rebate, a bead is worked around to top of the panels with a scratch stock – it is a small bead, so probably quicker this way than setting up a router.

The front of the frame oversails the front of the carcass to provide more of a purchase for fingers; it is bull-nosed after the handles are fitted.

After assembly and clean-up 75mm, 3in solid, drawn brass butt hinges are fixed in line with the internal rails.

While the lid is hinged the position of the handles can be marked off from the recesses in the carcass; the slots for the handles can then be gauged, squared round and cut out.

Semi-cylindrical inserts are split-turned, using paper in the glued joint between the two halves. After dividing the turning and cleaning up the face of the joint, the inserts are glued into their slots and the bull nose carefully planed and sanded down to them.

A 10mm, $^{3}/_{8}$in strip of padauk is glued, screwed and plugged to

Side elevation

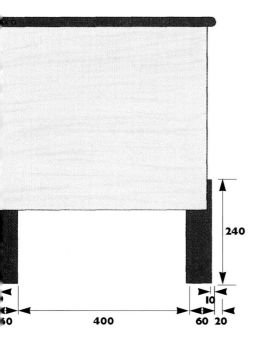

240

60   400   60 20   10

RETROSPECTIVE

We asked Rod Wales to tell us how he feels about this chest, designed several years ago.

"**LOOKING BACK**, something I try not to overdo, I feel the basis of this design still bears scrutiny, though it is certain that I would now make changes.

At the time I was largely concerned with the proportion and graphic elements of the composition, relating the three main parts – the lid, the box itself and the drawer – to each other, keeping them visually distinct yet unified, the whole exceeding the sum of its parts.

This, I feel, still works reasonably successfully – although I am not entirely convinced by the fluting which now seems rather uncertain, indeed I wonder whether it is necessary at all.

I would probably oversail the lid more definitely now, which would emphasise the step effect of the front elevation. I would certainly not use the lap dovetails – their purpose was to provide the ends with a contrasting detail to the front, but now I find them far too busy and self-important."

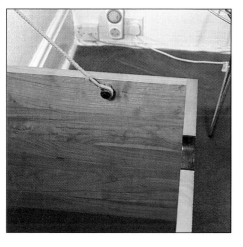

"Because this chest was intended for use as a toy box I made a skipping rope stay"

BELOW: Another split turning anchors one end of the 'skipping rope' stay...

LEFT: a turned button fixes the other

the short edges of the lid, providing a distinct line to the lid from the side and covering the haunched mortise and tenon detail.

Rope stays

Because this chest was intended for use as a toy box, I made a skipping rope stay. The 'handles' of the top are split-turned, then recessed for the rope and screwed to the underside of the lid, while two spigots are turned to take the loop at the opposite end.

The loop in the rope is finished with whipping twine.

The chest is finished with Danish oil and waxed, and the bottom of both chest and drawer is lined with felt.

BELOW: Neat buttons cover screw-fitted end capping

Writing slope

Peter Lloyd details step-by-step how he made this box

● **Former craft design technology teacher PETER LLOYD turned to making boxes at his home in Brampton, Cumbria after returning from teaching in Botswana some eight years ago. He specialises in jewellery boxes, work boxes and writing slopes constructed from woods like ripple ash, ripple sycamore and burr elm.**

PICTURE BY MARIANNE McALEER

ABOVE AND RIGHT: The completed box

NORMALLY I BUY wood when I come across it, and store it. I then either take a plank and decide on the sort and shape of box I can make from it or, if I have a specific commission, I'll see if I have timber to fit the bill. In this case the customer wanted spalted beech (*Fagus sylvatica*).

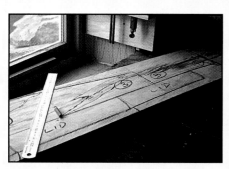

STEP 1) Mark out all the pieces of the box onto the plank, fairly oversize, making sure that the figuring runs around the box and that the lines of figuring don't clash with the lines of the box

With a plank of spalted beech finally run to ground and on the bench in front of me, I mapped out the writing slope, using a black wax crayon and a penknife.

With its feathered black lines and sudden changes of colour, spalted beech is beautiful, but if the 'spalting' has gone too far it can be soft so, before starting on the saw I had a dig with my knife.

STEP 2) Finalise the rough marking out; don't forget to check both sides. Without cutting the slopes on the sides, cut the pieces roughly to size

At this point I usually stand the pieces up on the bench. This helps to avoid missing one out.

STEP 3) Plane the bottom edges of the four sides square and straight, and shoot or plane the lengths precisely to size. Leave the widths oversize and the edges parallel

STEP 4) With an 8mm cutter in the router and the end grain to the fence, cut the stopped trench for the housings

I have a router bolted to a board and supported on an old school desk. The fence is pivoted at one end, and an arc-shaped slot at the other allows it to be adjusted. When I first set it up I found that the ash fence wasn't rigid enough. A heavy piece of angle iron screwed to the top solved that problem.

STEP 5) Cut the housings

I use wing-type slotting cutters mounted on an arbor for this sort of job, although when I first used this method I found that there was up to 0.5mm difference in the diameters of the cutters, so I had to send them all off to be sharpened to the same size. Now, with about six different-sized cutters and a handful of washers of various thicknesses, I can cut an almost infinite variety of housings.

STEP 6) Take a few shavings off the bottom of the sides and ends. This deals with any breakout which might have occurred

STEP 7) Rout the grooves for the base, shelves and top

Because of its stability, I use birch ply for the bases of most of my boxes. I also have a stock of 5mm ripple sycamore (*Acer pseudoplatanus*) which I use for shelves and trays. It's always preferable to cut the base slightly undersize – it would be disastrous if the joints failed to pull up at the end due to an over-large base.

STEP 8) Cut the base. Sand one side and cover the other with leather

STEP 9) Cut the shelves and sand to a fit for the grooves. Cut the shoulders allowing for some movement

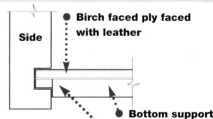

Side — Birch faced ply faced with leather

Bottom support

Bare faced tenon

STEP 10) Cut the groove for the front divider

Once again I used the end grain against the fence but this could be done using a mitre fence and stop. The position of the divider on this box was determined by the size of an A4 sheet of paper and my customer's wish to keep his business cards in the front of the box.

STEP 11) Cut the front divider and, unlike the shelves, cut a shoulder all the way round it

STEP 12) Make the bottom supports

The area of 4mm ply on this box should be supported underneath, *see fig 1* – I'd hate to think of its bottom sagging in 30 years!

STEP 13) FIGURE 1. The lid is a traditional mortise and tenoned frame with a flush panel inset. It has a slight taper from front to back to allow the back plenty of material to take the pivots without making the front look too heavy

STEP 14) Make the back pen tray in the same way as the lid panel, but leave the width oversize

The pieces for the lid should be arranged so the figuring in the wood is visually balanced, taking the handle into account. The inverted router was again put to use for the grooves and for cutting the lip on the edge of the panel. For the mortises I simply deepened the groove using a machine vice on the pillar drill, finishing off with a chisel.

The tenons were cut with a radial arm saw. Check the saw before cutting tenons as anything other than a 90° cut will result in time-consuming chiselling of shoulders, *see fig 2*.

STEP 15) Sand the back of the lid panel to 400 grit and glue up the lid

To avoid putting more pressure on one side than the other, use a band cramp rather than sash cramps. This avoids the problem seen in fig 3.

STEP 16) Once the glue has gone off remove the lid from the cramps, plane or saw off any excess and, having made sure the sides are absolutely parallel, drill for the pivots

Again I use a machine vice and the pillar drill. Check that the drill runs true to the edge of the lid before drilling, *see figs 4 and 5*.

STEP 17) Drill the sides for the pivot

To place these holes correctly, mark out lightly on the inner face of the side the position of the pen tray relative to the slope of the lid.

STEP 18) Cut two pivots

The pivots are made by starting with square section material, planing it to an octagonal section, then taking off the final corners with a chisel to acieve a round section.

STEP 19) Shape the pen tray and lid back and slot the piece together – because the lid is still slightly too wide the joints won't pull all the way up – check the lid stop and adjust as necessary

I used an 8mm bit for the lid pivot holes and an 8.5mm bit for the sides. I find that a lip and spur bit does a much better job than the more conventional machine bit.

STEP 20) The slopes can now be cut

STEP 21) Shape and sand all the inside surfaces and glue them up

One of these days I'll get to grips with gluing-up. I do everything right. I cramp the job up dry, I have all my cramps adjusted and ready to hand, I even take the 'phone off the hook – but I still manage to get my pulse racing and my grey hairs multiplying!

STEP 22) Fit the lid by planing or sanding, working from the pivot end downwards

Fitting the lid is very much a trial and error process. It must be perfect, and a piece of paper between the lid and the side is a good indicator of where it might need a fractional trimming.

STEP 23) Once the lid is in its final position, plane the slopes to about 0.5mm above the lid

STEP 24) Sand the sides down to about 120 grit then mark out and drill for the pegs

STEP 25) Sand the whole box to 400 grit

STEP 26) Cut the pegs in the same way as the pivots, having chiselled a slight taper, with a drop of glue in the hole tap them home and, with a sharp chisel, finish the ends with four facets

There's a very fine line between a peg that's tapered to make a snug fit after it's tapped in and one which is too large at the end and splits the wood.

STEP 27) Two or three coats of Danish Oil are followed by beeswax

STEP 28) Now the lid is finally fitted. A drop of glue and the pivots are pushed home, sawn and chiselled

This method of making a writing slope is in no way meant to be prescriptive. There is always more than one way of solving any problem. I think this method works, but pick out sections to use or adapt and, if they can be improved upon, share your discoveries with F&C. Above all, enjoy making boxes; there's nothing better than seeing a box emerge from the raw timber.

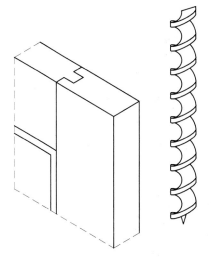

FIGURE 4. Check that the bit is parallel to the work before drilling

FIGURE 5. It might be a good idea to check the position of the pivot by using a piece of cord pivoted with a drawing pin.

FIGURE 2. A tenon cut with a radial saw which is not set at 90° will produce shoulder cuts like these.

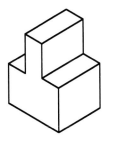

FIGURE 3. Sash cramps can push unevenly.

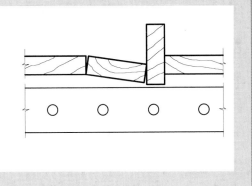

Hardy perennial

Andrew Skelton springs into action to make a garden seat

**ABOVE: Photo I
Garden seat in
Taun, ready for
painting**

PICTURE BY STEPHEN
HEPWORTH

DON'T BE FOOLED into
thinking that garden
furniture needs any less
careful design and making than
'proper' indoor furniture —
indeed the opposite is probably
the case.

True, hours of finishing to a
perfect sheen will not be
required, and the odd knot or
blemish will go unnoticed, but
for pieces destined for the
great outdoors raw joinery is
critical.

Glue will hold, but not forever,
and filler certainly won't. Rain

penetrates joints, frost expands
trapped moisture, sunshine bakes
and shakes surfaces, mould and
rot grow.

The effect of humidity and
movement on indoor furniture is
always a worry, but outside the
swings are from one extreme to
the other; the cycle is not
seasonal but daily — or more
frequent.

As if this battering by the
elements isn't enough, even we
humans treat garden furniture
more roughly than the indoor
variety.

Why bother?

So why bother? For a long and
trouble free life then we ought to
choose uPVC or metal, but
nothing compares with a wooden
seat. Visit any National Trust
garden and see a variety of often
charmingly eccentric seats.

Go to Grizedale forest — and
other sculpture parks — and
admire huge chunks of oak hewn
by sculptors like Jim Partridge.
Take a trip to Canary Wharf and
gaze in awe not only at the
design, but also at the number, of
Wales and Wales benches.

ABOVE: **Photo 2 Detail of back rail joints**

● **ANDREW SKELTON has been making high quality hardwood furniture for the past 15 years. He trained as an architect and says furniture-making is a natural progression from that discipline. He lives and works in the Derbyshire Peak District.**

PICTURE BY STEPHEN HEPWORTH

"Select good quality, sound timber and make good tight joints – for any weakness will be found out!"

Wooden outdoor seats can last — many longer than 60 years — but structural integrity depends on large and simple joints. Avoid joints and corners that collect water, and make sure that air can circulate to dry between members.

Select good quality, sound timber and make good tight joints — for any weakness will be found out!

Siting of outdoor furniture is all important, as is its maintenance. A seat under a shady tree in a damp corner is not going to last as long as a seat on a well-drained brick plinth in a sunny suburban garden.

A seat taken inside each winter and repainted or oiled, or just washed down each spring, has a better chance than a seat left to the weather all year. As with all furniture, the pieces that survive into future generations are the ones that are treasured and looked after; that some of these are well made and beautiful is often coincidental.

Design

Those people who are conservative in the home are likely to be even more so in the garden. This is not a criticism but an observation, and indeed the seat described here owes much to Georgian and Edwardian seats — almost anything with four legs, arms and a shaped back does! — and yet attempts a cleanness of line and economy of structure.

It is sturdy yet quick to make, but also, I hope, has sufficient individuality and quality to make the customer pleased to have gone to the trouble of having a seat made.　➤

BELOW: **Photo 3 Jointing of the arm to the front and back legs**

PICTURE BY STEPHEN HEPWORTH

"I have seen many tenons broken at over-zealous dowel holes"

I have used the end of this seat before with several variations of back, using both horizontal rails, as here, or a shaped top back rail and vertical slats. Slimmed down, it has also been the basis for one- or two-seaters — for

these make the legs 54mm, $2^{1}/_{8}$ in rather than 64mm, $2^{1}/_{2}$ in, and the rails 32mm, $1^{1}/_{4}$ in not 42mm, $1^{5}/_{8}$ in.

The tenons on the end seat rail, particularly at the front, are short; the arms and foot rail lock this load-bearing component in place.

I generally make the seat 450mm, $17^{3}/_{4}$ in from the ground to suit the average or tall person; this height is probably better for the elderly but may be too high for some. The seat height can be simply adjusted by shortening all of the legs, or alternatively the back legs only to increase the rake.

Timber

I have made many seats using oak but more recently I have favoured Papua New Guinea rosewood (*Pterocarpus indicus*) which has a natural oiliness and durability combined with impressive dimensional stability.

I obtain it from a supplier whose timber has been "produced in a way that is environmentally appropriate, socially beneficial and economically viable."
As this seat is painted, though, an oily timber is undesirable, so I used Taun (*Prometia pinnate*) from the same source.

Although I found it difficult to mortise, this dense timber machines well, is good to work with hand tools and to carve. Like many tropical timbers, the grain is rowed, and despite precautions the dust made me cough and sneeze.

The painted seat could well be made in softwood, particularly if it is given the 'double vac vac' treatment; in fact it may well outlast its hardwood contemporary.

Belt and braces

Other than some screws, pegged mortise and tenon joints are used in the construction of this seat. Make sure the dowels are made from strong, straight-grained timber, and use them where they are structurally appropriate.

Don't go drilling the joint away just to get a dowel in — I have seen many tenons broken at over-zealous dowel holes. I also like to glue my tenons with a polyurethane glue developed for boatbuilders. This cures with the moisture in the timber, can be used at low temperatures, and foams to fill voids at the bottoms of mortises and so on.

Drawings, templates

The end elevation and at least half of the back must be drawn

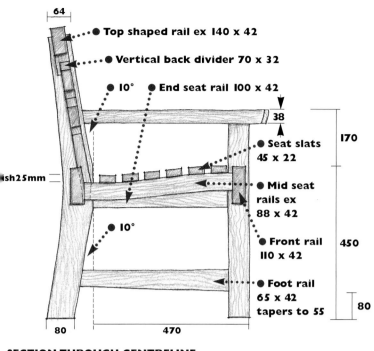

64

● Top shaped rail ex 140 x 42

● Vertical back divider 70 x 32

10° ● End seat rail 100 x 42

38

sh25mm

170

● Seat slats 45 x 22

● Mid seat rails ex 88 x 42

10°

● Front rail 110 x 42

450

● Foot rail 65 x 42 tapers to 55

80

80 470

SECTION THROUGH CENTRELINE

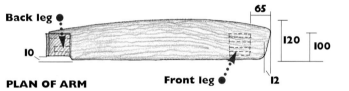

Back leg ●

65

10

120 100

PLAN OF ARM

Front leg ●

12

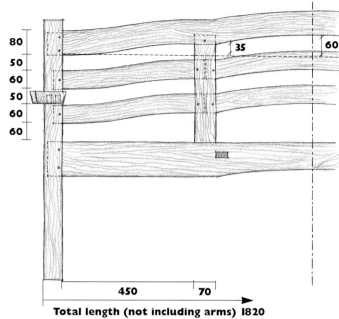

80
50
60
50
60
60

35 60

450 70

Total length (not including arms) 1820

FRONT ELEVATION

"The flat arms, ideal for placing a cool summer drink, are likely to suffer abuse as extra seating, so I pay particular attention to these joints"

carefully, full size, on a piece of board. I set up the outline of the drawing before making the templates for any curves needed to complete the drawing.

The four outer curves of the back step up towards the middle of the seat, and can be made either from wide pieces with square tenons or from narrower pieces with angled shoulders.

Either choice must be shown accurately, and the between-shoulder lengths of the three sub-rails plus two dividers must add up to that of the long rail, for this sort of section will not give however much cramping pressure is applied.

Joints

With all the parts planed and thicknessed, first shape the back legs, bandsawing off the waste and finishing accurately to the drawing using a hand plane, overhand planer or by making a template which can be followed by a router.

Mortise the front and back legs, remembering that the arms, seat and foot rails are horizontal and that the back legs must be propped up on the mortiser and carefully checked for alignment.

The flat arms, ideal for placing a cool summer drink, are likely

to suffer abuse as extra seating, so I pay particular attention to these joints. The front joint is a straightforward double tenon carefully dowelled to resist the stresses of lifting, *see photo 4*. The back joint is a tenon and housing joint with a screw though the outside of the arm into the leg, *see photo 5*.

Cut this joint with square shoulders, paring the angle by employing a chisel and guide block, *see photo 6*.

Finish the arm by running a bevel on the inside edge and tilting the bandsaw table to saw the outside curve — leaving the front square until after assembly makes cramping up easier.

Stub tenon

The joint for the two mid-seat rails is designed to take the weight of the sitter and stop the front and back rails bowing outwards without weakening the rails too much.

So a hefty stub tenon carries the weight and a through wedged tenon locks the rails, *see photo 7*.

The mortises on the back and front rails need to be opened up to take the wedges for, if wedges are used just to close the gap rather than to create a dovetail, the joint is not worth the trouble. ➤

LEFT: Photo 6 Using an angled block to pare the back shoulder on the arm

"There is plenty of potential for mayhem at this stage"

The two vertical dividers of the back are tenoned into the top rail and housed and screwed into the angled bottom rail. I cut the housing with a router fitted with a guide bush using an MDF template, *see photo 8.*

Cramping mayhem

With all the joints cut and fitted, the edges can be chamfered or rounded to taste — but be careful to stop at the few flush joints. Before cleaning up the components mark the position of the dowels with a bradawl, as they can be difficult to sight quickly when the marking-out lines have gone.

The back and front are assembled first and require long or joined cramps. If the sub rails have been cut accurately the back should only require two long cramps and two smaller ones to pull up the vertical dividers.

G cramps can be used to apply pressure to the housing joints. The back can be cleaned up and dowelled when the glue has set.

Because the screws are very awkward to reach when the arms are on, now is the time to dry fit the seat rails and screw on the seat slats. Stainless steel or brass screws will make later slat replacement easier.

Gluing and cramping cross-framing is no easy task, but Balcotan glue claims to have an open time of 75 minutes!

I lie the back of the seat on my bench before applying the glue, then knock the rails into the front which has been placed on a blanket on the floor. The front is then lifted and turned and the tenons located in the back — there is plenty of potential for mayhem at this stage.

As the end rails are now vertical they are relatively easy to cramp; the seat is turned upright before cramping the arms down to the front legs. The mid rails must be cramped and wedged before a well-earned cup of tea is allowed.

Clean up, dowel the joints, plug the screw holes, and the seat is ready to receive the finish of your choice — if any. ◼

SUPPLIERS

THE TIMBERS mentioned are obtainable from the Ecological Trading Company, 659 Newark Road, Lincoln LN6 8SA Tel: 01522 501850

Balcotan polyurethane wood adhesive is available from Melco Bonding Supplies, Hillview, Park Road, Nailsworth, Gloucestershire GL6 0HZ Tel/Fax: 01453 833985

"A piece of veneering that may be done well in 10 minutes will be done badly in an hour"

Regency sofa table

F&C Editor **Paul Richardson** on a classic piece of furniture

THOUGHT OF AS a Regency furniture type, the sofa table actually appeared towards the end of the eighteenth century. Gradually superseding the Pembroke table from which they were developed, sofa tables are named after their intended purpose. This is to stand against a sofa, which also dictates their elegant proportions – longer and thinner than the squarish Pembroke, and usually fitted with two drawers rather than one.

They are also as close to a 'sampler' of cabinetmaking techniques as I have come across. Carcass-making, drawer-dovetailing, rule and finger joints – use a turned stretcher and, with the veneering and shaped legs, pretty much everything is covered in one project.

What really lifts these versatile pieces of furniture into a class of their own is the approach to the legs. A Pembroke stands on fine tapered legs which suit the delicacy of the design, but which would look plain on the longer and more substantial sofa type. Instead, end standards – or sometimes single pedestals – support the carcass. This is an opportunity for some very stylish work.

Veneers and veneering
The veneer used for this example, one of a pair, is from my dwindling stock of Brazilian rosewood (*Dalbergia nigra*) which, together with mahogany (*Swietenia sp*), satinwood (*Fagara flava*) and maccassar ebony (*Diasporus ebenum*) is contemporary with the design. These are less than environmentally friendly even as veneers, so figured sycamore (*Acer pseudoplatanus*) could be used, and a crown cut walnut (*Juglans sp*) makes a convincing faded mahogany if bleached. Stain sycamore grey and it becomes 'harewood' in Georgian parlance, likewise rosewood is 'palisander' and maccassar ebony 'coromandel'.

All veneering is carried out using ➤

PHOTOGRAPHY BY
DENNIS BUNN

COLOUR ILLUSTRATIONS
BY IAN HALL

Scotch glue and a hammer. Any other method may be used, of course, but I recommend hot glue as it is not only in period but is suitable for both flat and curved work. Remember to sponge the veneer with near-boiling water an hour or two before use, laying it between two flat boards to 'tame' it.

To further prevent buckling, brush glue onto the groundwork and the top of the veneer before hammering down. The trick is to move fast, not allowing the glue to gel – a heated iron can be used on large areas, but a piece of veneering that may be done well in 10 minutes will be done badly in an hour.

When joining veneer that is being laid with Scotch glue, overlap the pieces and cut through both with a sharp knife for a perfect fit.

Table top

The top of this piece is constructed from 15mm MDF, lipped at the rule joints and veneered on both sides.

First the groundwork is prepared, cutting the MDF to size and applying the lipping, *see fig 1*, with size '0'

biscuits or a cross-grained loose tongue. Templates for the radius of the table top's corners and the inner radius of the crossbanding may be made from offcuts.

Backing veneer is applied to the underside of the table top, and the pieces are laid veneer-side down on newspaper to prevent bowing. The main body of the face side is veneered with the grain running across the width, leaving the edges overlapping the area to be crossbanded.

With a cutting gauge set to the width of the crossbanding these edges are trimmed, the corners being cut with a sharp knife from the small radius template. The crossbanding is then applied.

Rule joints cause much consternation, but with matched cove and round-over cutters for the router they present no problems. The trick is to pay careful attention to the pivot of the hinge, *see fig 1*, cutting the rounded part of the joint first and adjusting the fit with the cove.

With the hinges fitted, trim the edges of the top and round the corners from the larger radius

template. Either a scratchstock or router can be used to cut a channel for a boxwood (*Buxus sempervirens*) line which should be left slightly proud and sanded flush when dry. All that remains to complete the top is to crossband the edges and sand to a finish.

Carcass construction

This type of carcass may be used for all those tables with drawers of which the Georgians were so fond. If the corner blocks are extended down as tapered – or turned – legs, then you will see the basis for a Pembroke; omit the recess for the flap supports and you have a writing table.

All parts are mahogany except where they might be worn by the drawers, in which case they are oak (*Quercus robur*); thus back, sides, divider and corner blocks are mahogany, drawer rails, muntin and runners are oak. The Georgians would perhaps have used Baltic pine (*Pinus sp*) where I have used mahogany.

Cut the mortises for the single-shouldered tenons into the corner blocks, then work the back and

FIGURE I – THE RULE JOINT

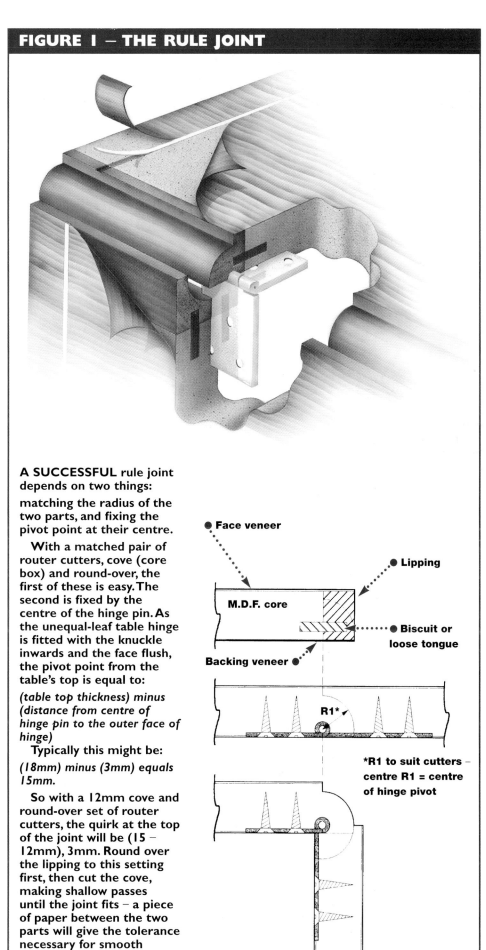

"I normally allow 30 minutes to veneer the carcass including cleaning up"

sides' tenons to fit. The back may be glued to its corner blocks at this point.

It is my practice to cut the shoulders for the dovetails on the front rails from a stop on the radial arm saw, then the dovetails themselves using a simple jig on the bandsaw. On such a small construction any inaccuracy will send the job out of square, so all parts must be exactly matching.

The sockets are marked from the tails with a knife and cut to depth. The drawer muntin is fitted next – not forgetting to work a 6mm groove in the back edge of this piece before assembly – using a double mortise and tenon. The front rails and corner blocks may now be glued up.

Glue the sides and divider to the front and back, then fit the drawer runners, again marking the sockets from the dovetails – where these form a joint with the drawer rails, they should be half lapped.

When all is dry, the outside of the now complete carcass should be cleaned up, making sure all joints are flush, and the veneer prepared as previously described.

A SUCCESSFUL rule joint depends on two things: matching the radius of the two parts, and fixing the pivot point at their centre.

With a matched pair of router cutters, cove (core box) and round-over, the first of these is easy. The second is fixed by the centre of the hinge pin. As the unequal-leaf table hinge is fitted with the knuckle inwards and the face flush, the pivot point from the table's top is equal to:

(table top thickness) minus (distance from centre of hinge pin to the outer face of hinge)

Typically this might be:

(18mm) minus (3mm) equals 15mm.

So with a 12mm cove and round-over set of router cutters, the quirk at the top of the joint will be (15 – 12mm), 3mm. Round over the lipping to this setting first, then cut the cove, making shallow passes until the joint fits – a piece of paper between the two parts will give the tolerance necessary for smooth operation.

● **Face veneer**

● **Lipping**

M.D.F. core

● **Biscuit or loose tongue**

Backing veneer ●

R1*

*R1 to suit cutters – centre R1 = centre of hinge pivot

"I have occasionally seen the evidence of an over-long or zealously countersunk screw causing a pimple in the table top"

Cut the crossbanding for the rails and false drawer side as accurately as possible – about 1mm oversize – and also eight rectangles for the corner blocks.

With two bookmatched pieces for the false drawer fronts to hand, veneer the carcass. Glue will try to go everywhere when crossbanding the rails, and this must be cleaned up as you go, for if it is left to dry it will take hours to remove neatly.

It is important to work as quickly as possible. I normally allow 30 minutes to veneer the carcass, including cleaning up.

When the veneer is dry inlay a boxwood line around the false drawer fronts, then sand to a finish and set aside until assembly.

Drawers

The hand dovetailed drawers are entirely traditional with mahogany fronts on oak linings and, as this subject has been frequently and exhaustively covered elsewhere, I will simply point out that the veneering is carried out after the drawer has been assembled but before the bottom is fitted. Fit the drawers to the carcass and make any adjustments before applying the boxwood line, thus avoiding any reduction in its width.

Finger joints

If anything, finger joints are an exercise in careful marking out, the object being to achieve a large wooden hinge. As with rule joints, the pivot point is the crucial factor, *see fig 2*.

Traditionally these were made from beech (*Fagus sylvatica*), but as this is the diet of choice of the woodworm – any restorer will tell you – these are mahogany.

When making batches of these I use a sliding box jig on the table saw, but as only four are needed for this project it is probably as quick, and certainly more satisfying, to cut them by hand. On completion of the carcass they are screw-fixed from inside.

End standards

The style of end standard used for this piece is simple in form, but post-Georgian experience tells us that this is the weak point of the sofa table. Select the uprights from straight-grained mahogany, but cut the legs from a piece which follows the curve as closely as possible as any short grain here will be asking for trouble.

Prepare a ply or MDF template for the legs remembering to allow for the sliding dovetail. It is best to cut this joint line straight and square first, and even to work the dovetail, before bandsawing to shape as a large bearing surface is helpful.

My favourite approach to these is to set up a dovetail cutter in an inverted router, first cutting the female part. Without adjusting the height of the cutter, by judicious adjustment of the fence the male part may be cut to a high degree of accuracy – taking a little off each side and checking the fit in the mating part.

After bandsawing I finish the profile of the legs with an inverted router, fitted with a bearing trim cutter running against the template, pinned to the work. This involves some cutting against the grain and is a little nerve-wracking – the job may instead be done with spokeshave and rasp.

The uprights must be veneered and bound before the standards can be glued up. Veneer the faces first, then trim the veneer to the edges while it and the glue are moist. The edges can then be cross-banded without waiting for the faces to dry.

The boxwood binding is fitted into a rebate cut into the corners of the standards with a bearing-guided router cutter. Glue the binding with PVA, carefully wiping off any surplus and holding in place with taut masking tape. When these parts have been sanded, glue up the sliding dovetails and fit the plates which 'block out' the base of the upright.

Veneer and bind the legs in the same way as the uprights, then mitre the moulding around the top of the leg blocks. After cleaning up fit the castors.

Laminating stretchers

The arc stretchers shown here are laminated in mahogany, although any straight grained timber will do as the whole is subsequently veneered. Five laminates is about right for this radius, which should be made around a former of a slightly tighter curve than that required as the finished laminate will spring slightly when the clamps are removed.

As an alternative a turned stretcher is entirely appropriate for this piece – if you choose this option, the turning should be spigoted into the centre of the blocking out at the base of the end standards. The sofa table as a form has been widely used, and most books on antique furniture will provide ideas for variations.

Assembly

French polishing should be carried out before the now completed sub-assemblies are put together. The precise polishing process will vary according to the veneer chosen, but if a stain or any but the palest of pale polishes is used the boxwood lines must first be masked with a carefully applied line of clear polish, then scraped clean before the final rubbers. My client had asked that these tables should not look too new, so rather than distress them we deliberately introduced a 'dirty' polish.

To assemble, lay the table top face down on a soft blanket and fix the carcass to it with screws through the top drawer rails and runners. I have occasionally seen the evidence of an over-long or too zealously countersunk screw causing a pimple in the table top so exercise caution.

The standards are fixed to the carcass with screws from the inside; the stretcher is then screwed and plugged to the standards and the bottom of the central drawer runner. ■

● **Full dimensioned drawings and cutting list for this piece are available free to readers of F&C. Please send a stamped, self-addressed A4 envelope to: Sofa table drawings, Furniture and Cabinetmaking, Castle Place, 166 High Street, Lewes, East Sussex BN7 1XU.**

FIGURE 2 – THE FINGER JOINTS

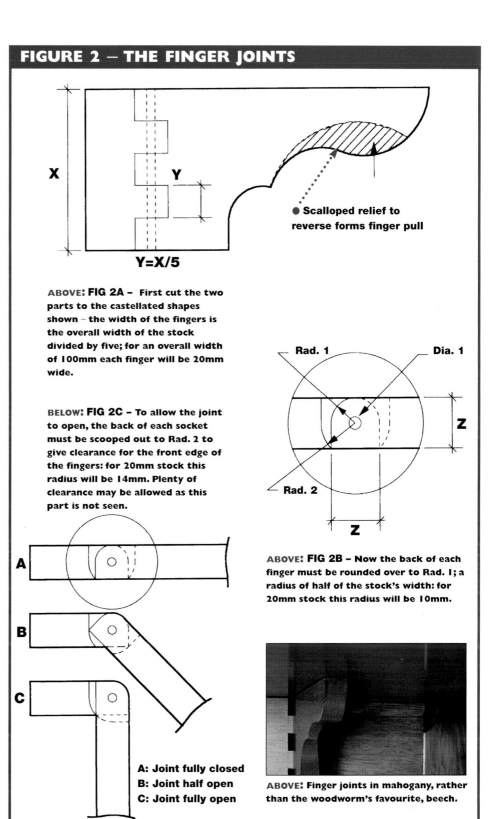

Y=X/5

ABOVE: **FIG 2A –** First cut the two parts to the castellated shapes shown – the width of the fingers is the overall width of the stock divided by five; for an overall width of 100mm each finger will be 20mm wide.

BELOW: **FIG 2C –** To allow the joint to open, the back of each socket must be scooped out to Rad. 2 to give clearance for the front edge of the fingers: for 20mm stock this radius will be 14mm. Plenty of clearance may be allowed as this part is not seen.

ABOVE: **FIG 2B –** Now the back of each finger must be rounded over to Rad. 1; a radius of half of the stock's width: for 20mm stock this radius will be 10mm.

A: Joint fully closed
B: Joint half open
C: Joint fully open

ABOVE: Finger joints in mahogany, rather than the woodworm's favourite, beech.

FINALLY THE hole for the pivot pin, Dia. 1, must be drilled. This must be exactly centred on the stock, and half the stock's thickness from the ends of the fingers: for our example this distance is 10mm. Drill this hole with the joint assembled and correctly lined up to ensure smooth operation - drilling half way through from each end minimises any run-out. Match the drill's diameter to the available pin - a five-inch round wire nail works well.

PHOTOGRAPHY BY STEPHEN HEPWORTH
ILUSTRATIONS BY ANDREW SKELTON

> "Although I have not hung out the 'Maker of Edwardian Repro Shield-backs' sign, I will certainly agree to the next such job that comes my way"

Squaring up to

Andrew Skelton shares his anxieties about making a shield-back chair

● **ANDREW SKELTON** has been making high quality hardwood furniture for the past 15 years. He trained as an architect and says furniture-making is a natural progression from that discipline. He lives and works in the Derbyshire Peak District.

I HAVE TO start this article by confessing that I'm worried about writing it: on the one hand this is clearly not a project of stunning contemporary design and on the other I know very little about the detail of reproduction furniture.

So the description that follows is not an authoritative 'how to do it' but more about how I approached copying a chair and the lessons — mostly positive — that I learnt on the way.

This Sheraton-style shield-back is, I guess, Edwardian and not of any great value. The clients had five chairs and required a sixth to make up the set; unable to find anything remotely matching, they asked me to make one.

I saw it as a challenge for it is difficult to make a single chair

profitably and besides, I had never made a chair like this. I realise that this example does not exhibit the fine subtleties of a genuine Sheraton chair, but what interests me are the basic shapes and methods of construction.

Prejudice

At the time I was asked to make this copy I was struggling with the design of a chair, *see fig 1*, and welcomed the opportunity to look at something different. I have never liked the Sheraton and Hepplewhite period; because of that prejudice I confess I have never really looked closely at the design or construction of their furniture.

The idea of the chair I was making was to try and use just five pieces — two back legs, two front legs and a seat. Here was a

chair, I thought scornfully, that used 15 pieces, not to mention the corner blocks and the upholstered seat.

On closer inspection, however, my admiration for the Sheraton chair grew as I began to understand its logic, economy and elegance. In truth I failed to make the simple five-piece chair — the seat alone is made up from three pieces, the back from difficult to make tapered laminates; and the joint between the seat and the back is a nightmare.

What surprised me most about making the reproduction of a reproduction was that I really enjoyed it. Perhaps it was not having to worry about the design; although I have not hung out the 'Maker of Edwardian Repro Shield-backs' sign I will

LEFT: Photo I Marking the back leg template

RIGHT: The finished chair, right, pictured with the original

BELOW: Photo 2 Morticing for the back foot rail

ıeraton

RIGHT: Fig I Andrew Skelton's oak chair

certainly agree to the next such job that comes my way — there is so much to learn from how other people do things. ▪

Drawing

I am a drawer of furniture — not a mock-up maker or a start-and-see-how-it-goes maker but a sort-it-out-on-the-drawing-board maker. I did not, however, want to draw this chair, firstly because it would take so long, and secondly because I had a perfectly good full-size mock-up that I thought I ought to use.

If I wasn't going to draw the chair then I had to try and sort out some way of getting started.

It all seemed to be compound curves, and I needed to start with some square timber and cut the joints by machine — surely something somewhere was

square to something else?

Clearly the front legs are square to the seat plane, and after a bit of measuring I found that the massive 90 by 60mm ($3^1/2$ by $2^3/8$in) blanks for the back legs are also square to the seat, *see fig 2*.

Only two templates were needed — one for the back leg profile and one for the shield — plus a card pattern for the vase back splat.

Back legs

To find the shape of the back legs, I put a piece of MDF on the seat, asked a helper to hold another piece at right angles to it, *see fig 2*, and against this placed a third piece on which I marked the pattern of the back leg, *see photo 1*.

The profile of the back leg now ➤

**ABOVE: Photo 3
The basis of the
chair**

**ABOVE RIGHT:
Photo 4 Marking
the shield on the
back assembly**

became clear. The section over
the seat joint is square to the
seat; above it — the shield
portion — is a straight taper and
below it the leg sweeps back in a
curve.

This chair produces a great
deal of waste; although the
components could be stacked so
that several could be bandsawn
from a large board, machining
the curved parts would
necessitate sophisticated jigs, and
for the sake of speed I was keen
to avoid making these.

I reckoned that the chair I was
copying had been largely
machine-made, but I also decided
that in order to make the jigs the
first chair would have been made
pretty much as I was doing.

Joints

In order to do as much work as
possible while the components
are still square, and having
planed the taper over the shield,
all the back leg mortices are cut.
These mortices are at an angle to
the leg blank to take account of
the top-to-bottom taper of the
back legs.

When cutting angled joints it is
my practice to make angled
wedges that save having to alter
fences from square; thus a single
wedge can be used on the saw,

with the morticer and the tenoner
giving consistent and accurate
angles.

When morticing for the foot
rail the back leg is set at a jaunty
compound angle, *see photo 2,*
with a wedge beneath it for the
taper, and a second wedge to
give the backward sweep of the
leg.

As can be seen from the
photos, to achieve the inside
faces of the back legs a large
proportion of the blank must be
removed. With these cut and
cleaned up and the complicated
— but extremely elegant —
splice joint for the bottom of the
shield prepared, the rails can be
jointed.

I took the dimensions of the
crest rail and foot rail from the
original, cut their joints and
assembled them between the two
back legs. The shoulder length of
the seat rail and the bottom
shield rail can then be taken
directly from this assembly.

Performing these tasks for the
front is recreation by comparison
— strange to think that such a
light chair develops from such
hefty beginnings, *see photo 3.*

Shaping, moulding
The template for the shield is
made by simply tracing around

the original and using to mark
out the back assembly, *see photo
4.* The shapes are then bandsawn
from their blocks.

Keep the waste from the first
cut and stick it back on with
double-sided tape in order to
mark out and balance the parts
when cutting in the other plane.
Hanging on to the waste will
help with holding the shapes in
the vice at a later stage.

On this chair the back is
concave, meaning that the crest
rail, bottom shield rail and vase
splat are hollowed. The crest rail
hollow is bandsawn from its
45mm (1³/₄in) block and, as the
curve on the bottom rail is only
slight, it can be spokeshaved.

To shape the face of the vase
splat I routed a series of grooves
from the middle to the outsides,
each cut becoming successively
shallower. Using a block plane, I
merged these cuts to a smooth
curve and planed the back to
follow it. But before hollowing
these parts the joints for the splat
need to be cut.

Dreaded splat
One of those 'this is how you
make a chair' books would have
come in handy for this part. My
solution was difficult but worked
in the end. ➤

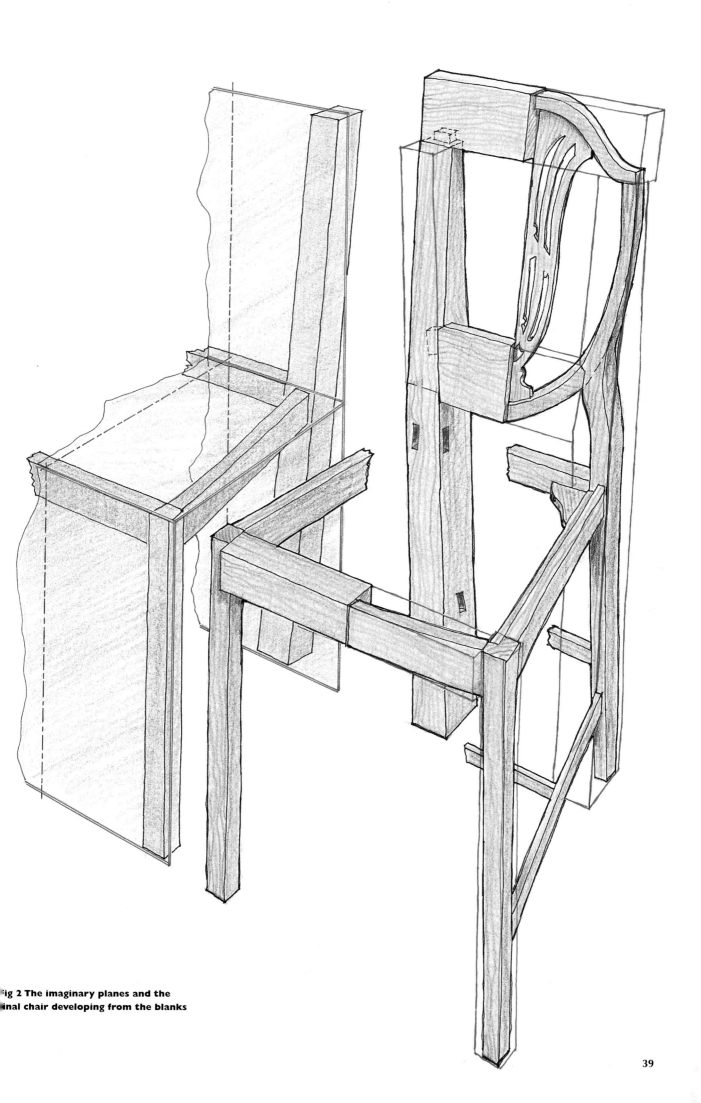

Fig 2 The imaginary planes and the final chair developing from the blanks

"I am a drawer of furniture — not a mock-up maker or a start-and-see-how-it-goes maker but a sort-it-out-on-the-drawing-board maker"

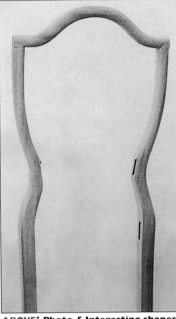

ABOVE: Photo 5 Interesting shapes

On the bottom of the splat I put a short stub tenon with shoulders scribed to the bottom shield rail – the shallow mortice and tenon are not affected by the final hollowing and are thus relatively straightforward.

In order to allow for some movement the top of the splat is let into a groove the full thickness of the splat. This groove follows not only the shape of the shield but the concave shape of the crest and splat.

Using a bearing-guided slotting cutter in a table-mounted router, I cut the bottom mortice and as much as I could of the top groove. The curve of the top groove is chiselled out by hand and the splat gently planed to fit.

So far I had felt challenged by the compound shapes and appreciative of the sense of the construction but the vase back splat and its carved decoration mystified me.

I should have done some research into the meaning of the decoration and perhaps I will yet. In my ignorance the carving looks like an upside-down foxglove, a handkerchief held up by five drawing pins supporting three eggs, an unidentifiable flower and a handful of wheat ears.

Cleaning up

Now all the components can be cleaned up and shaped. The curves seem to be designed for the smooth flow of spokeshaves and merge gracefully into one another while the shaping and rounding over of the back is natural and logical, *see panel*.

Seat, foot rails

Dowels are often used for the side seat rails, but if using mortice and tenon joints then one or other must be at an angle for the taper. As I was using a single-ended tenoner logic dictated that the tenons and their shoulders should be angled.

Here again a wedge — exactly the same as that for the taper of the back legs — allows the angles to be repeated simply and accurately.

I tenoned the seat rails first and assembled the chair so that I could measure the shoulders of the foot rail.

A taper on the inside of the front leg as well as the pronounced curve of the back legs complicate these shoulders.

To find the shoulder length of the cross foot rail, the chair must be assembled again before being taken apart for cleaning up before final gluing.

Modern blocks

One glance at the modern corner blocks will prove that this chair was not made 80 or so years ago. I struggled and scraped knuckles putting in slot head screws in corner blocks — Pozidrive, deep-threaded, gelatimo-coated screws are one of the great joys of the modern workshop.

Whether this chair matches the rest of the set will depend more on its final colour and appearance than the actual making. Staining and polishing not being my strong point, I left these processes to an expert. ■

WEGNER'S WISHBONE

ROUNDING THE back legs, I sensed that I had seen these extravagant shapes in another guise, *see photo 5*. I realised that they were very much the same shapes as the designer Hans Wegner used in his Wishbone Chair, *see fig 3*.

Now I am not trying to suggest that Wegner copied this shape, either consciously or sub-consciously, but am merely remarking that here, on my bench, were shapes that had truly excited and delighted me.

Interestingly they were parts of a chair type that I had seen often and to which I was indifferent. How little we see when we are prejudiced! For those who are worried, Wegner's chair legs are bent before being machined, so making the piece immensely strong and light.

To make the half-round beads and the shaped section between them I dug out my scratch stock and ground and filed a cutter. The scratch stock was surprisingly easy to use; when the grain became too steep I carved the moulding with a chisel and a few gouges, assembling the back before carving the corners of the beads and merging the mouldings over the shield.

Fig 3 Hans Wegner's Wishbone Chair

Apothecary's chest

Kevin Ley takes a calculated risk with burr elm

PHOTOGRAPHY BY
STEPHEN HEPWORTH

I LOVE THE challenge of working in burr elm (*Ulmus procera*). There is an element of risk, and as with certain other potential objects of beauty, the desired result can only be achieved with a careful approach!

I have made several of these chests using various contrasting woods for the carcass, and up to 14 drawers with burr fronts, but this speculative piece made for a museum, *see panel*, is the first in solid burr throughout.

Design

This piece is loosely based on the apothecary's chest of pre-NHS times; the stylised drawer attachment both adapts its function and improves balance and interest.

It also makes use of the availability of small pieces of burr, and gives me the welcome opportunity to make plenty of drawers.

Making panels

Time and care spent marking out and making the panels has a profound effect on the end result. The distinctive grain pattern of the burr makes joins difficult if a patchwork quilt appearance is to be avoided.

Try to book-match sequential boards, or mask the join by flowing the grain and colour through it. Blemishes can be put on the inside or made into a feature!

Before gluing up, cut the pieces over-size, mark them carefully, and lay them out to see how they relate to each other.

The top and drawer fronts should have the best figure. While each will be a picture in its own right, it must relate to the whole to give an overall pleasing effect.

If, as a result of the wild grain, there is end-grain along the joints, strengthen them with a loose tongue.

Drawer frames

Burr tends to move more than most other woods, so allowances must be made for this in the construction.

The main movement is across the grain, and as the grain in the top, sides and base is more or less running in the same direction, there should be little problem. The drawer rails, however, run across the grain. ➤

> "The distinctive grain pattern of the burr makes joins difficult"

● On leaving the RAF in 1987 KEVIN LEY set to turning his hobby into a commercial proposition. The former squadron leader designs and makes bespoke furniture from his cottage and workshop in Shropshire.

ABOVE: Careful matching of boards for the top and drawer fronts

ABOVE LEFT AND RIGHT: Cramping up has to be done in sequence

"Allow plenty of time – in the words of David Savage this is not a Friday afternoon job"

RIGHT: The formal design contrasts with the wild grain of the burr

Do not glue the mortise and tenons at the back of the frame; leave a 3mm, $^1/_8$in gap to allow for expansion and contraction.

Make the frames 1mm, $^3/_{64}$in wider at the back than the front to allow for easy drawer movement. For the same reason the drawer spacers should be tapered front to back by 1.5mm, $^1/_{16}$in each side; fit them very carefully, and cut the mortises for the front uprights between the drawers.

Construction

Cut the sides to size, and slot to receive the frames and back. Do as much of the final filling and finishing as possible before assembly.

The first stage in the assembly of the carcass is probably the most difficult as the drawer frames must be glued into the sides, and the uprights between the rails, at the same time.

Only the front and back rail ends should be glued into the side slots, to enable the dry joint at the back to run smoothly.

Do a trial dry assembly to check everything, prepare the clamps and equipment, and above all allow plenty of time. In the words of David Savage this is not "a Friday afternoon job".

Check the diagonals back and front to ensure all is square; leave to set. Indulge in a little cheating allows fitting the uprights first, using a plugged screw with which to pull up the joint, then fitting the frames to the sides.

ABOVE: Drawer detail

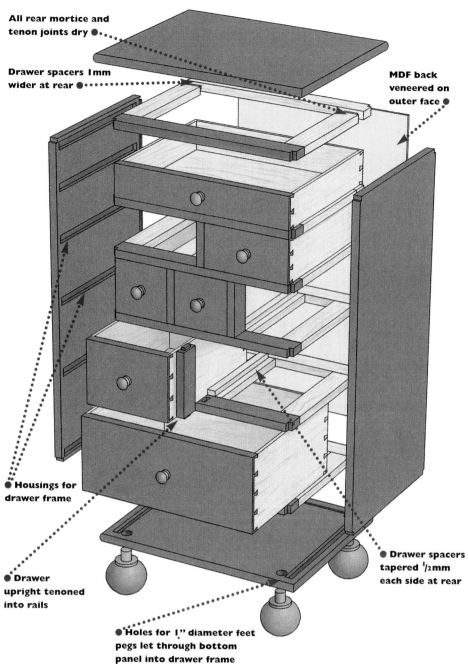

All rear mortice and tenon joints dry ●

Drawer spacers 1mm wider at rear ●

MDF back veneered on outer face ●

● Housings for drawer frame

● Drawer upright tenoned into rails

● Drawer spacers tapered ¹/₂mm each side at rear

●'Holes for 1" diameter feet pegs let through bottom panel into drawer frame

Top, base, back

Cut the top, base and back to size, allowing the extra 1mm width at the back; slot the top and base to receive the sides and back.

I use suitably faced 5mm MDF for the back, and glue it in all round for extra strength.

Rounding over the edges of the top and bottom protects them from chipping and provides a nice highlight to the finish.

Clamp up, check for square and leave to set.

Drawers

The drawers are constructed in the normal way. I always use cedar of Lebanon (*Cedrus libani*) for the linings, and cedar-faced MDF glued in all round for the bases, again for extra strength.

The smell of cedar is wonderful, it repels insects – and attracts customers!

When preparing the drawer fronts keep them a tight, tapered fit to allow for adjustment when fitting; finishing the inside faces at this stage is easier than doing it when the drawers are assembled.

When dovetailing the fronts, keep tools razor-sharp and pressure-light; the wild grain entails cutting both with and against it, and the work is all too easily chipped. As a last resort keep the Superglue handy!

Fit the drawers a little looser than usual; to minimise any visual effect with the shadow line, set them back about 1mm from the front.

"The old oil adage of 'once a day for a week, once a week for a month and once a year thereafter' is not far out"

Knobs, feet

Taking advantage of more odd lumps of leftover burr, I chose bun feet, adopting a similar shape for the knobs. Again, the rounded surfaces show off the oiled finish nicely.

The pegs which fit the knobs and feet are better made as loose dowels from a suitable straight-grained timber, and glued in. If turned from solid burr with an unkind grain they can snap.

Finishing

A Danish-oiled finish is the best choice; it brings out the deep richness of the grain pattern and colour, and is improved with time and tender loving care. The burr can be quite porous, and oil penetrates well into the wood, helping to stabilise it.

The old oil adage of 'once a day for a week, once a week for a month and once a year thereafter' is not far out.

➤

ABOVE: Sharp tools and care are needed to avoid chipping the burr

The first coat is liberally applied, left to soak in, and refreshed every 15 to 20 minutes until it will take no more – four to six coats. Wipe it off with a soft cloth, allowing no oil to build up on the surface, and leave it to harden for 24 hours in a warmish, dry place.

The surface is cut back with a Scotchbrite grey pad, and further light coats applied every 24 hours until the desired effect is achieved.

Ensuring that there is no build up of oil on the surface, the last coat can be cut back and buffed with a soft cloth, or waxed and buffed.

Future care amounts to an annual light coat of teak oil.

The inside surfaces of the burr should also be oiled in a similar way, but not those in contact with the moving surfaces of the drawers; these should be sealed by a thorough waxing.

Stunning impact

The inherent instability of burr may mean a slight sacrifice of engineering tolerances, but this minus is far outweighed by the plus of its stunning visual impact.

Close tolerances do not necessarily feed the soul, but the beauty of this wood does. A piece of burr furniture lives, it has visual – and actual – movement, and is lent a natural beauty by virtue of its instability.

Burr makes a fitting tribute to our devastated elm trees, so good luck to those who venture a piece in this lovely timber. ■

ABOVE: Feet and knobs are turned

RIGHT: Oak blanket chest with Egyptian-inspired hinged closure

A photo of an Ancient Egyptian shrine inspired **Guy Lewis** to make a small oak chest with a wooden strap-hinge assembly

Hourglass figure

THE WORK of designers like Ambrose Heal and Gordon Russell, who often incorporated wooden latches, catches and other mechanisms into their pieces, has long since fascinated me.

This chest borrows these ideas and is very simply constructed from four flat, angular panels and a thick slab top to achieve a waisted, hourglass shape.

Inspiration came from a photograph of an Ancient Egyptian shrine, but others recognise Japanese and mediaeval influences.

Made throughout of English 'stripey' and brown oak (*Quercus robur*), the wooden hinge assembly is also fumed, *see panel.*

Slab top

The measurements for the box are dictated by the 50mm (2in) thickness of the slab lid, which for added stability is constructed from two 25mm (1in) boards; I was lucky enough to buy some very nicely figured quarter-sawn, partially brown oak that was planked up at 32mm (1¼in).

For the 535 by 345 by 50mm (21 by 13 by 2in) top, make up two boards of 560 by 370 by 25mm (22 by 14 by 1in) and glue together to make up the thickness. Leave the boards to

dry for 24 hours.

Cut the top to size, giving a 60° angle to the slope. All the cut faces are veneered with a 2mm (¹⁄₁₆in) oak facing, the off-cuts from the top being used as cauls. Veneering the edges in this way will conceal the edge of the laminated top, instead emphasising the desired solid slab appearance.

When the angled edges are cleaned up they become sharp and unfriendly. I used a small radius round-over bit in my router to soften them,

preferring to guide it along a straight edge rather than use the guide-bearing – which would not work adequately in this case, due to the fall-away of the edges. ➤

● **GUY LEWIS is a professional cabinetmaker working in Sturminster Newton in Dorset. He can be contacted on 01258 471642.**

PHOTOGRAPHY BY JOHN MORLEY

LEFT: The strap which forms the rear leaf of the hinge runs through the underside of the lid

ABOVE: Chopping in for the brass hinges – carefully

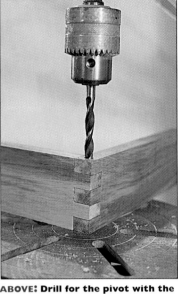

ABOVE: Drill for the pivot with the hinge assembled but not rounded, from both sides

BELOW: The chest has an elegant side profile – note the upward curve at the end of the closure

"I find rough-cutting on the bandsaw and trimming up to a pencilled line with the router along a straight edge is much quicker to set up and just as accurate"

This is all very laboured but worthwhile.

Box construction

The boards for the front, back and sides are now cut to size from 19mm (^{3}/4in) stock. First cut the front and back, using the lid to work out the measurements for the tapered sides.

I find rough-cutting on the bandsaw and trimming up to a pencilled line with the router along a straight edge is much quicker to set up and just as accurate as using the sliding table on my sawbench.

Radius the ends of the front and back panels to soften the edges.

The sides are cut to a size and shape dependent on choice of joint – I used routed stopped-housings, although I'm certain a biscuit jointer would do as good a job.

Before assembly, rebate the bottom of the sides so that the baseboard can be attached.

This is made from 10mm, ^{3}/8in stock which is glued and screwed into the routed rebates and reinforced along the underneath of the front and back panels with glued and screwed battens.

Strap-hinge assembly

The wooden strap-hinge assembly is made from 25mm, 1in stock which runs from front to back through the top. Prepare

a board 610 by 80 by 25mm (24 by 3 by 1in) thick and cut it into two to measure 260 and 360mm (10 and 14in) long.

The hinge requires an odd number of knuckles – I chose five; divide both pieces by five and mark up accordingly. Mark the depth of the knuckles – this must be the same as the stock's thickness.

Carefully remove the waste between the knuckles, ensuring that they fit closely. I make the knuckles using the excellent Woodrat to guide a router, but use any method that works, from a saw and chisel upwards.

To ensure accuracy in making the hole for the hinge-pin, check the vertical alignment of the pillar drill. Mark the central axis of the knuckles on both sides. Using a compass, mark on both sides the radius to be put on the knuckle ends.

Assemble the wooden hinge at 90° and drill the hole, meeting in the middle from both ends to minimise 'run-out'.

I use 10mm (^{3}/8 in) brass rod for the hinge-pin.

Fettling knuckles

With the knuckle-joint assembled at right-angles with the pivot pin in place, radius the ends of the knuckles with an inverted belt-sander or similar, as near to the previously marked line as

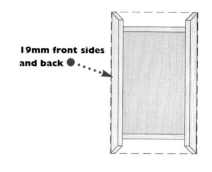

19mm front sides
and back ●·······

530mm

●· ·● Sides
inset 25mm

● 10mm bottom boards

340mm

50mm

400mm

38mm

ABOVE: Elevations

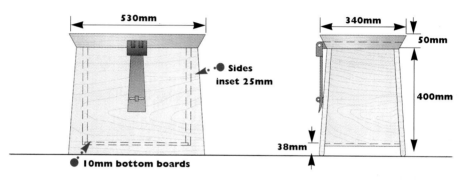

● Diameter 10mm brass hinge pin

● 25mm x 75mm hinge
housed in lid of box

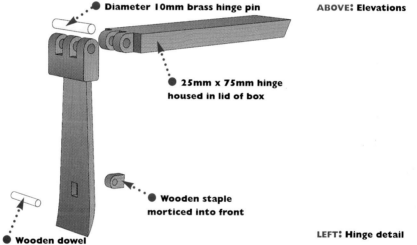

● Wooden staple
morticed into front

● Wooden dowel

LEFT: Hinge detail

possible; reassemble the other way around and repeat the procedure until an element of hingeing is apparent.

Carefully fettle the knuckles with the joint disassembled until they hinge through 180° with no resistance. This involves constant disassembly and reassembly, but patience is rewarded at this point as the joint will break if forced and will be slack with visible gaps if too much is removed.

Mark out the shape of the moving part of the hinge in both planes, and chop the square hole before moving on to the bandsaw. With square edges providing stability, cut the tapered thickness first, then stick the offcut back on with masking tape before cutting the sides to shape. Clean up with the help of scrapers, drum sanders, etc. until an even and smooth surface is produced.

Routing housing

Rout the housing in the top to receive the long part of the wooden-hinge, again taking care to ensure a snug fit.

My over-worked Elu MOF96E router has to remove a large amount of material during this operation, so I proceed very slowly, taking many passes and gradually increasing the depth. Battens clamped on either side of the housing act as a safety stop

should my attention wander during this nerve-wracking procedure.

The hinges are now fitted to ensure that all components marry up.

Mortise and dowel

With the hinge assembly, lid and box fully assembled, mark through the hinge flap's square hole onto the front panel the position of the mortise that will accept the wooden staple.

Chop the mortise very carefully as it is at this stage that much hard work can be ruined.

Make the wooden staple then fettle it to fit the square hole, using a belt-sander or similar to gradually round the end until the hinge assembly clears without fouling the staple.

A wooden dowel as a closure not only looks good, but makes opening the chest more involving; so fashion one to go through the staple and drill a hole for it.

Finishing

After the staple is glued in to the front panel, the chest is disassembled for the last time to enable finishing to take place. After sanding and checking for dents and scratches – these can often be removed with the aid of an electric iron and a damp cloth – the chest is first treated to an application of a mixture of linseed oil and white spirit which is left on for at least 24 hours; then an even coat of shellac sanding-sealer is brushed on sparingly and left overnight; treatment with 0000 wire wool ➤

Simply fuming

I COLOURED this particular chest's wooden-hinge assembly by using .880 ammonia solution. Ammonia is dangerous stuff and should be used with caution, *see F&C 5 for safety tips.*

The chemical does, however, alter the colour of oak pleasingly, is very controllable and enhances the grain well.

I carry out small-scale fuming in a cardboard box sealed with masking tape, making a temporary air-tight polythene tent for large pieces.

Once fumed, keep the hinge-assembly well away from the chest until it is sealed to avoid the danger of the rest of the chest being affected.

ABOVE: An oak pin neatly completes the closure

LEFT: The knuckles of the hinge are rounded on an inverted belt sander

> "Battens clamped on either side of the housing act as a safety stop should my attention wander during this nerve-wracking procedure"

and wax polish, with three or four further coats of wax completes the finishing procedure.

A leather thong threaded through two holes in the side and knotted, secured by a grooved dowel in a hole in the lid, restrains the heavy lid from opening too far. All of these holes should be drilled after finishing.

The chest can now be assembled for the last time, and the thong fitted for length, before applying one last coat of wax for luck. ◼

BELOW: A variation with drawers

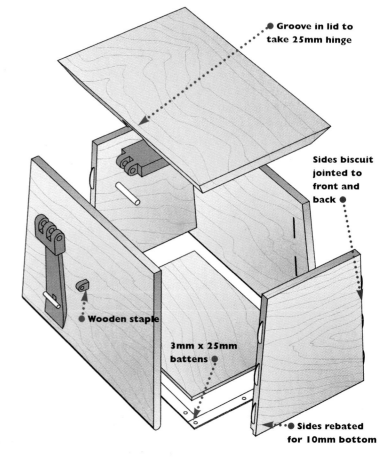

● Groove in lid to take 25mm hinge

Sides biscuit jointed to front and back ●

● Wooden staple

3mm x 25mm battens ●

●● Sides rebated for 10mm bottom

Mark Griffiths took on a challenge when he agreed to make a display cabinet with curved glass doors; here he describes the experience

Curved space

● **MARK GRIFFITHS** trained at Brighton College of Arts and Technology when he underwent a three year City & Guilds apprenticeship in furniture making and design. After specialising in restoration work he turned to furniture making, and now runs his own workshop at Barcombe, East Sussex, where he fulfils commissions for mainly locally based clients.

IT WAS ONLY on leaving the clients' house that I realised just what I had talked myself into making, and I felt that queasy sensation in my stomach. These were two of my best customers, however, and all of the previous work I had carried out for them had started as a challenge, but given me immense satisfaction when completed.

Simple brief

The brief was simple; a display cabinet to show a collection of cut glass. They had once seen a cabinet with turned rosewood (*Dalbergia nigra*) columns, and wanted this idea incorporated into the piece. The cabinet was to fit into a corner of the lounge where one wall meets a staircase, this having a lovely curved corner. It was this feature that inspired me to suggest that a cabinet with curved glass would look interesting − I should know better.

I was to curse myself for this for the next few weeks; a normally sized cabinet with a curved glass door would be tricky enough, but this was to be a little over eight feet tall to match the height of the staircase, and only 18 inches or so in its widest section.

Thus followed days of drawing and talking to glass merchants, metal frame-makers and other cabinetmakers, the conclusion of which was that to make the cabinet with just one single door would prove to be far too costly. If this were done a one-off metal frame would have to be constructed to take the glass, onto which the rosewood surround would then be clad.

The immense weight of this, especially when the door was open, would give rise to wall fixing

problems. Consequently it was decided to make three separate doors, with two dividing rails.

Templates and rods

With this type of job the first step is always to make as many rods – full-size plan drawings on a sheet of, say, hardboard and templates as possible; these are invaluable to check that the work is true and accurate. With hardboard rods the work can be physically laid out on the rod to check the accuracy of curves and joint lines, for example.

Templates of each curve are also made and checked against the rod to be used as guides for the router work. In addition, a rod which shows the full length of the cabinet is used as a constant reference guide, so avoiding cumulative errors creeping in.

When the materials being worked with are expensive and time is in short supply − as it always is! − it is important to have good, clear and accurate full-sized rods to work with if costly mistakes are to be avoided.

Curved glass

The cabinet is constructed mainly around the glass. Originally I had been told by a glass merchant that I would have to use 10mm, $^3/_8$in thick glass; this would have made each door incredibly heavy, which I wanted to avoid.

On sending out an order for the glass to another merchant, along with a hardboard template of the curve I required, he told me that the doors could, in fact, be made from 4mm, $^1/_8$in thick glass. This shows that it is always best to shop around to make sure you are getting the best advice.

The reason that having glass curved to shape is so expensive is that a former must first be made of the particular shape, onto which a sheet of glass is laid and heated until it 'flops' around the mould. It is therefore a good idea to ask the glass merchants to hold onto the former, at least until the job is fitted, just in case another piece is needed!

Turnings

The turned sections of the carcass and door sides are turned to a diameter of 40mm, $1^5/_8$in. The stock for this is laminated from rosewood machined to 40 by 25mm, $1^5/_8$in by 1in and beech (*Fagus sylvatica*) machined to 40 by 15mm, $1^5/_8$ by $^5/_8$in.

These two sections are then jointed with '0' size biscuits along their centres to give a 40 by 40mm, $1^5/_8$ by $1^5/_8$in squared section ready for turning (*see picture*). This ensures that only the rosewood will be seen from the outside, and when the door is opened the beech will match the blonde, interior wood.

As I am not a turner, I had the turning for this piece carried out by a local woodturning firm which is equipped with a copy lathe. Resorting to a specialist in this way makes sure that the diameter is consistent throughout the length of each section − vital as each complete length is made from three sections, jointed together with dowels.

Carcass

The cabinet back is made from 18mm, $^3/_4$in thick MDF to give strength and stability. This is veneered in ripple sycamore (*Acer pseudoplatanus*) which, with its

"It is
always best
to
shop
around to
make
sure you
are getting
the best
advice"

ABOVE: The finger pulls are just visible.

LEFT: Mark Griffiths rises above his difficulties.

ABOVE: The compound curve of the cornice requires care when veneering.

RIGHT: View from above.

"I often have to resort to 'washing' the veneer in warm water and washing up liquid"

ABOVE: The doors are fitted with piano hinge.

RIGHT: The turnings are produced from a rosewood and beech laminate, biscuited for added security.

creamy white colour, gives a striking contrast to the rosewood and allows the coloured glass to be displayed at its best.

With the turnings finished and the carcass backs sanded, the next stage is to fix the turnings to the sides. First mark and drill the dowel holes in the edges of both sides and the turnings. The sides' edges are then routed, with an 18mm, ^{3}/4in core box cutter, to create a concave 'bed' for the turnings to sit snugly in .

Plinth and cornice

The plinth and cornice are made using a slightly over-sized template of each required curve. This is an opportunity to use up some of the MDF offcuts which clutter up the workshop, as the curves are built up brick-fashion from small sections of this material cut to the required radius.

When dry they are trimmed to shape using another, actual size, template as a guide. I used a spindle moulder for this, but a router or even a sanding disc or belt could do the job. MDF is an ideal medium for this type of work, but beware the fine dust it produces and wear a good mask or respirator.

The veneering of these components is best done with contact adhesive, which is particularly good for veneering rosewood which can otherwise cause problems due to its oily characteristic. When laying rosewood using Scotch glue, I often have to resort to 'washing'

the veneer in a solution of warm water and a small amount of washing up liquid, which helps to neutralise the oil.

Even then some rosewoods are stubborn, so the best plan is to lay as much as will go down and leave the work overnight to dry. The next day the blisters are still there, but with gentle heating with an iron and some warm water, they should settle.

When using contact adhesive on end grain MDF, it is always important to apply two coats due to the absorption rate of MDF. Both plinth and cornice are cross-grain veneered, which is straightforward for the plinth because it is curved in only one direction.

The cornice, however, has a compound curve, which means that the veneer must be cut into equal segments, i.e. imagine the peel of a quartered orange which would follow the curves. Having a dry run at this can be a wise precaution to make sure that all the segments align.

Carcass assembly

The plinth and cornice are now sanded and fitted to the carcass. The cornice is made up as a frame, which is biscuited to the top of the sides, and a 6mm, ^{1}/4in rebate is routed on the inner edge to take a piece of glass.

This allows the viewer, when at the top of the stairs, to look straight down through the cabinet and glass shelves. Obviously this could be omitted if the cabinet is to be placed in the corner of a room.

The two door dividing rails, made

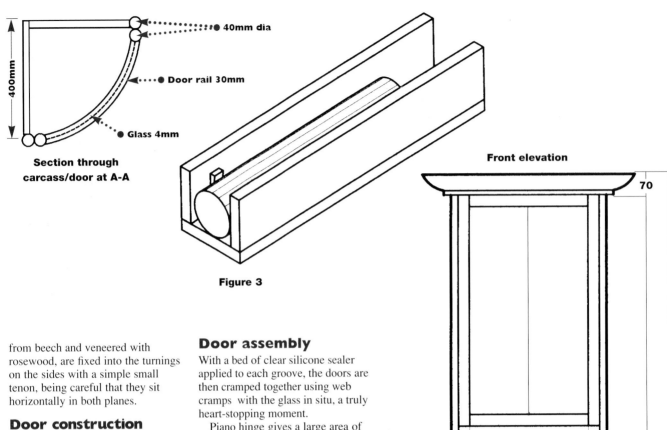

400mm

• **40mm dia**

← • **Door rail 30mm**

← • **Glass 4mm**

Section through
carcass/door at A-A

Figure 3

from beech and veneered with
rosewood, are fixed into the turnings
on the sides with a simple small
tenon, being careful that they sit
horizontally in both planes.

Door construction

The next stage is to make the doors.
This was something which I put off
for as long as possible, due to my
weak heart – the glass alone for each
door cost well over £100.

Using the rod, work out the
position of the turned side rails of
each door and rout a groove along
the inside length of each to take the
glass. This is done using a simple
holding box (*see diagram above*)
which may also be used when
dowelling the turnings together.

Constructed in melamine-faced
MDF, it gives a good sliding surface
on which to run the router and fence.
The turning can be held in place in
the box either by means of pins or
screws inserted in the sides or, as I
used here, small wedges. The routed
groove is then flared out on the inner
edge, using a chisel, to the angle at
which the curved glass enters. Again,
this is determined by offering the
glass up to the full-sized rod.

The top and bottom rails are next
cut using a template and bearing-
guided cutter on a router table. They
are then cross-grain veneered in
rosewood, sanded and fitted to the
radius of the stiles. Each rail is then
jointed to the turned door stiles using
10mm, ^{3}/$_8$in dowels.

Although each piece of glass is
created over the same former, they
will all prove to be slightly different
in their curvature. Therefore, each
groove in the top and bottom rails
must be marked out using the glass
as a guide, and routed out by hand.

Door assembly

With a bed of clear silicone sealer
applied to each groove, the doors are
then cramped together using web
cramps with the glass in situ, a truly
heart-stopping moment.

Piano hinge gives a large area of
support and keeps the doors, with
their awkward shape, sitting
correctly in the carcass. If this is
used a 12mm, 4^3/$_4$in flat should be
routed on the hinge-side turnings of
door and cabinet to give a location
for fitting the piano hinge. Again the
holding box can be used for this.

Discreet magnetic catches, the
type that fit neatly into an 8mm,
^{5}/$_{16}$in drilled hole, are the most
suitable catch for this situation.
With the magnet fitted to the door
frame, all that is needed on the
inside of each door is a countersunk
screw head.

Handles on this cabinet would be
a problem, so this is overcome by
cutting small finger pulls into the
sides of each door. To do this drill
three 10mm, ^{3}/$_8$in holes close together
and use a gouge to blend these
together. This will be invisible to
the eye when looking straight onto
the cabinet, but just visible from
one side.

I used a rosewood spirit stain to
correct some discrepancies in colour
between the solid and veneered
rosewood, then finished the whole
piece with Danish oil and clear wax.
Danish oil always looks particularly
good on turned work.

Making this piece of furniture was
a nerveracking experience, but
extremely rewarding when
completed. As always, the best part
of a job is standing in the clients'
home, with the furniture installed
and the customers satisfied. ∎

Front elevation

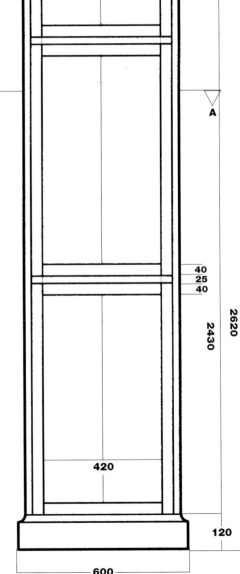

70

A ◁   ▷ A

40
25
40

2430

2620

420

120

600

Andrew Skelton
viewed with diffidence the making of a box without specific function, then said "why not?"

● **ANDREW SKELTON** has been making high quality hardwood furniture for the past 15 years. He trained as an architect and says furniture - making is a natural progression from that discipline. He lives and works in the Derbyshire Peak District.

Domed box

MOTIVATION IS ONE of the most difficult aspects of working on my own. Orders arrive erratically, cash coughs and splutters rather than flows, and my enthusiasm comes and goes.

The most problematical time is when a large job is finished and delivered..Even with the paperwork up to date, some designing done and a day off taken I find it hard to get stuck in to the next piece.

A friend told me that he tried to take a week between major pieces for experimentation, so I decided to give myself a gentle lead in by making something small and different – a box I could produce quickly and which might serve as a prototype.

Constraints

I decided that the box had to be made quickly out of what was available in the workshop; it should, as far as possible, avoid conventional cabinetmaking techniques, so no dovetails or hinge-sinking; each part should have a structural use, employing as few components as usual – so the bottom is not a floating solid panel but MDF glued to the sides to provide strength.

At first I was a little uneasy about making an object to serve no particular purpose. However, a look around the house at bowls filled with fir cones and at jugs of dried flowers put my mind at rest; making something that was essentially just a pleasing object seemed justifiable – if it could contain pebbles or a few old coins then so much the better.

Reference points

I have always loved boxes and chests with domed lids and bound with metal straps or studded with rose-head nails; they speak of medieval reliquaries, treasure chests or those wonderful Arts and Crafts Movement chests.

The stainless steel in my box suggests these models, and I was fortunate in having suitable laminating formers to hand to produce a curved lid. The ripple sycamore (*Acer pseudoplatanus*) used has a lovely pattern, but this is greatly enhanced by the curvature. ➤

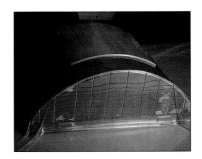

"In retrospect, the use of narrower housings and shouldered stub tenons would have been better"

LEFT: PHOTO 1
The lid is laminated in a vacuum-bag press.

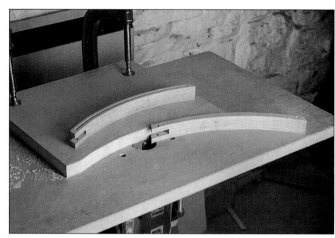

ABOVE: PHOTO 2 Shaping the sides using a simple template and a bearing-guided cutter in an inverted router.

ABOVE: PHOTO 3 Routing the groove in the oak curves – note the simple bandsawn fence.

"I needed several goes and some hard planing to achieve a good fit"

The laminates

The laminates for the curves were bandsawn from mild timber, carefully keeping them in sequence, and then thicknessed so that seven laminates made 15mm, $^{19}/_{32}$ in. A galvanised steel band tightened by a screw thread pulls the glued laminates round the former in my jig.

The lid panel is made from three layers of 1.5mm, $^{1}/_{16}$ in

birch ply with ripple sycamore veneers on both sides – the outer plies should have their grain direction at right angles to the face veneer.

This sandwich can be vacuum-pressed in one go, with any joins in the top and bottom veneers lined up, care being taken to ensure the whole is square on the mould, *see photo 1*.

One glue mix, *see panel*, should do the laminates, the lid and veneer the bottom. I veneered the upper face of the bottom only – a panel this small doesn't seem to need a balancing veneer – and tried to match the lid and bottom veneers.

Corner joint

For the corner joint a routing was housed in the sides the full 10mm, $^{3}/_{8}$ in width of the back and front. In retrospect, the use of narrower housings and shouldered stub tenons would have been better.

Rout the groove for the bottom, stopping it within the housing; then tackle the corresponding rebate on the bottom. The healthy glue line from an accurately fitting bottom will add greatly to the strength of the box.

To shape the sides I used an MDF template, pinned into waste at both ends, and a bearing guided router cutter, *see photo 2*.

The top edges of the back and front are angled to the curve of the lid panel and trimmed to fit the ribs, *see fig 1*.

Hinge slots

With the oak ribs cleaned up and

Section and elevation of side

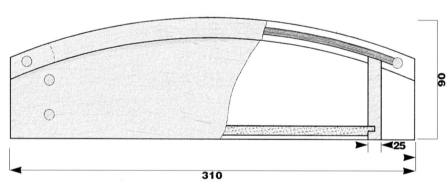

310
90
25

Elevation of front

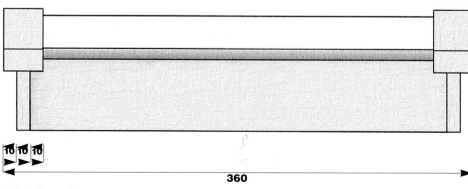

10 10 10
360

FIG 1 Elevations.

LEFT: Sycamore figure is enhanced by the curve of the lid.

BELOW: PHOTO 4 Cutting the lid panel.

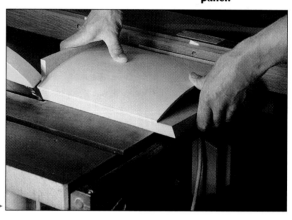

left slightly over-length, mark and cut the hinge slots; these are carefully chiselled back to fit the profile of the sides.

With the sides left in position, the 6mm holes for the two stainless steel rods are accurately marked and drilled in what is the most critical part of the project.

Run the groove for the lid panel with a 5mm router bit – a tight fit for the veneer and ply sandwich – using an inverted router and a simple bandsawn fence. The first 6mm hole is lowered over the router bit and the groove stopped at the second hole, *see photo 3*.

Lid panel

Now the lid panel needs cutting to size; its width is determined by the now glued-up base and its length by the distance between the stainless steel rods.

Ideally the panel should bottom out in the groove in the oak ribs; for the hinge to work it must be cut accurately.

This curved panel presents a few problems, and my solution involved simple jigs plus trial and error. I measured the width from the central join on my veneers, and drew lines from these to which I bandsawed and planed.

Place the panel, on edge, on a flat surface and check it with a square. To cut the panel to length I made a jig with a base, a block to fit the curve, a fence and a square edge, *see fig 2 and photo 4*.

With the saw blade tilted to the appropriate angle, run the square edge against the fence cutting the

base of the jig. Put the panel in place, score the bottom veneer to prevent it spelching out, and cut the panel.

Screw a stop to the cut edge of the jig, replace the panel, adjust the saw fence and make the second cut. I needed several goes and a some hard planing to achieve a good fit.

To ensure that the panel fits snugly to the rods I put a slight hollow in the edge of each end, accomplished by packing out the router table with a scrap of MDF ➤

First cut

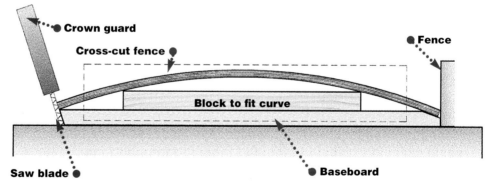

Crown guard

Cross-cut fence ●

● Fence

Block to fit curve

Saw blade ●

● Baseboard

Second cut

Stop screwed to baseboard ●

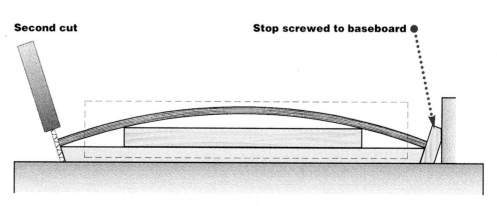

FIG 2 Jig to cut lid panel.

ABOVE: Elegant hingeing arrangement integral to the box's design.

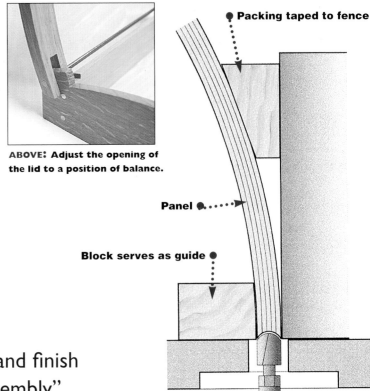

ABOVE: Adjust the opening of the lid to a position of balance.

Packing taped to fence

Panel

Block serves as guide

FIG 1 Jig to rout hollow in edge of lid.

"A purist would probably mask and finish each component before final assembly"

secured by double-sided tape, and running the panel carefully over a cove bit, *see fig 3* – a process that is easier than it sounds.

The lid can then be

ANOTHER ANGLE

THE AIM OF this project is to suggest an approach rather than defining a method.

For those without suitable moulds for the curves – the ones I used had been made for a large project and had already produced several hundred bends – it would seem rather excessive to build them for a box.

There are obviously many ways of approaching this project depending on the availability of equipment such as the vacuum-bag press used here; it would be possible to cut the ribs from solid timber and cooper the panel from a number of small, angled slats.

assembled and, when it is cramped up, checked for fit against the base.

Base to lid

When the glue has set join the base and lid with the hinge rod, and use a sharp plane to trim the ends of the laminated ribs flush with the ends of the sides.

The back of these ribs may need adjusting by trial and error to enable the lid to open to a position of balance.

With the lid removed again, the holes for the stainless steel dowels are drilled before a final clean-up.

I sprayed the completed lid and base, although a purist would probably mask and finish each component before final assembly.

Finally, glue in the polished stainless steel rods and dowels with epoxy – placing the box somewhere warm will ensure that the glue cures.

Mathematically ship-shape

Bill Clayden's dome-lidded chest has a pronounced maritime flavour

I DESIGNED AND made this piece for two prime reasons, the first being totally self-indulgent – I simply wanted to make a chest with a lid with double curvature, partly for its appearance and partly for the technical challenge.

The second reason was down to the acquisition of some interesting figured yew (*Taxus baccata*) from which to make beautiful panels to complement a cupboard with two slabs of yew for doors.

For design inspiration I looked to the styles of makers like Alan Peters, John Makepeace and James Krenov.

Shaping up

The overall size of the piece is that of a medium-sized tool chest, the carcass shape being determined by adding the width of the frame to the square panels, resulting in a pleasing double cube.

The shape of the lid was determined by sketching curves to produce a double curvature top. While a curved lid cannot be covered so easily with domestic clutter, the shape does mean it won't be too comfortable to sit on.

I have always admired the visual effect of a traditional yacht's cabin ceiling, displaying closely spaced planks and exposed beams.

The self-indulgent element includes influences from early years as a shipwright apprentice and from later years as a result of a mathematical background, and results in each plank being about 4mm ($^5/_{32}$in) wider than its neighbour on the outside.

Frame construction

The joinery for the frame is straightforward, the rails being fitted to the corner posts with secret haunched tenons and the muntins tenoned into the rails. Two stretchers across the bottom are dovetailed into the bottom ➤

PHOTOGRAPHY BY
JOHN CLEAVE

"While a curved lid cannot be covered so easily with domestic clutter, the shape does mean it won't be too comfortable to sit on"

TOP RIGHT:
Photo 1 Yew and
cedar panels are
glued and
cramped

MIDDLE RIGHT:
Photo 2 Lid frame
components

BOTTOM RIGHT:
Photo 3 Plank
laminations
clamped to a
former to follow
the curve of the
lid

rails, which are rebated to house the bottom boards.

The frame is made with ash (*Fraxinus excelsior*) carefully selected from a nominal 50mm (2in) rift-sawn honey-brown board.

The corner posts are selected to display growth rings roughly parallel to the diagonal of the cross-section, thus ensuring that the figure on the post, when viewed from the side and the ends, is similar to the growth rings spaced fairly closely together, *see Timber Selection panel*. Where possible, when selecting the rails the slight curve of the figure is used to echo the curve of the lid top.

Cut the mortices, the tenon shoulders and the cheeks. The frame is first assembled dry without the panels, and the surfaces of the joints are cleaned up apart from final sanding as the presence of the flush panel makes final trimming difficult after the panels have been inserted in the frame.

The inside edges of the frame are radiused and stopped with a curve centred on the middle of the corner panel radius. Most of the waste is removed with a router, and the corners are finished with a chisel, file and sandpaper.

Side, end panels

The side and end panels are composed of an inner layer of 6mm ($\frac{1}{4}$in) cedar of Lebanon (*Cedrus libani*) and an outer layer of 8mm ($\frac{5}{16}$in) yew cut from a nominal 25mm (1in) thick board with one waney edge. The light-coloured sapwood is in spectacular contrast to the much darker heartwood.

The boards are ripped, planed, and glued to yield a panel of the required size, with a streak of sapwood running from top to bottom to provide a bookmatched effect.

The panel is cut to the exact size, with the sapwood centred to resemble another muntin. The edges are radiused with a router and the corners radiused.

The yew panel has a clearance of roughly 4mm ($\frac{5}{32}$in) to give the required effect of a close-fitting panel while allowing for slight movement across the grain.

The inner layer of cedar of Lebanon is glued up from narrow boards to produce a slightly oversize panel. The radiused edges of the yew panels and the

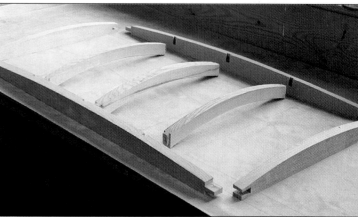

exposed outer surfaces of the yew and cedar panels are finished and polished before being glued together with Cascamite, *see photo 1*.

After removal from the clamps the outer edge of the cedar is sawn to size and the remainder of the panel sanded. The outside is sealed with one coat of diluted polyurethane varnish and wax polished. The inside is lightly wax polished.

The frame is glued up with the panels in place, using PVA glue for the mortice and tenon joints. The panels are not glued in the frame apart from a small dab at the top and bottom of the middle

of each panel to allow it to move symmetrically in the frame across the grain.

Bottom

The bottom consists of solid 14mm ($\frac{35}{64}$in) thick cedar of Lebanon laid parallel to the side for maximum strength, with loose tongues between the boards, *see fig 1*. The boards are fitted to the rebated bottom rails and held in place with battens screwed to the rails.

The boards are pinned in the middle to allow for the small amount of expansion and contraction, and to prevent overall movement. The boards

directly above the stretchers are glued to them so as to make the bottom stiffer. Again, the insides of the boards are just lightly waxed.

Lid

The lid frame is made of ash of a paler shade than the carcass frame, *for construction see photo 2*. The corners are dovetailed with the tails worked on the short ends to take advantage of the strength provided by the boards glued to the top of the frame. The tops of the sides and ends, and the beams are formed by arcs of circles.

The beams are cut from the solid and dovetailed into the sides. Ideally the beams should be cut from timber grained to follow the curve.

Mark out from a full-size drawing the top edges of the frame, and bevel. After the frame is glued up any minor adjustments to the bevel may be easily seen by clamping a thin lathe over the top of the frame and removing any high spots with a plane or file.

Planking

The planks – as in the boat-building sense – covering the top are composed of two laminations, ash on the outside and cedar of Lebanon on the inside, *see fig 2*.

The use of two laminations has two advantages: firstly, the planks may be permanently bowed to fit the frame very closely, so avoiding any distortion which might arise due to springing a solid plank into position; secondly, it enables the outside to match the ash frame and the inside to match the cedar lining of the carcass.

To add visual interest, the

width of the planks follows an arithmetical progression from the outside to the centre, each plank being 4mm ($^5/_{32}$in) wider than its neighbour, *see panel*.

The solution allows all the planks to be cut from 50mm

(2in) stock because as the planks near the edge and become narrower they need more curvature to lie snugly on the beams while retaining edges which are parallel to the side of the chest. ➤

ABOVE LEFT: Photo 4 The shape of the strip's edge is marked with dividers

ABOVE: Photo 5 Clamping the planks to the frame

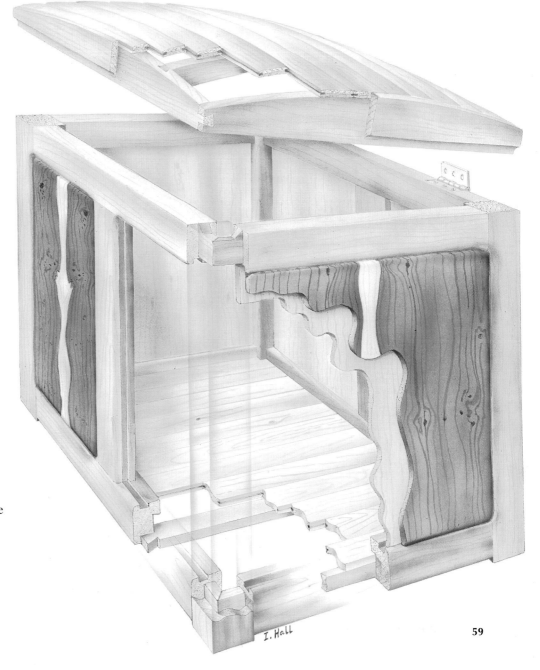

I. Hall

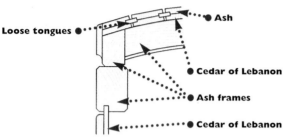

Loose tongues ●···· ····● **Ash**

●···· **Cedar of Lebanon**

●···· **Ash frames**

●···· **Cedar of Lebanon**

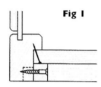

Fig 1

Two stretchers are glued to 3rd & 6th boards & dovetailed into side rails ●

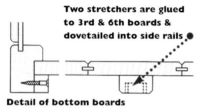

Detail of bottom boards

TIMBER SELECTION

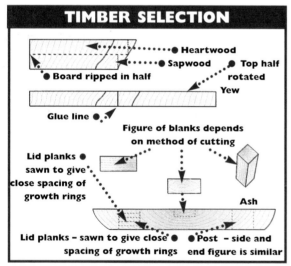

●···· **Heartwood**
●···· **Sapwood**
● **Top half rotated**
Board ripped in half
Yew
Glue line ●·

Figure of blanks depends on method of cutting

Lid planks ●
sawn to give
close spacing of
growth rings

Ash

Lid planks – sawn to give close ● ● **Post – side and spacing of growth rings**   **end figure is similar**

The planks are cut from the same ash board as the frame of the carcass, and are sawn from the plank to give closely spaced growth rings rather than the florid figure which would have resulted if the planks had been merely ripped parallel to the edge of the plank.

Laminations

The laminations are glued up with Cascamite over a former shaped

ARITHMETICAL PROGRESSION

THE STRIPS are joined by 4 by 12mm ($^5/_{32}$ by $^{15}/_{32}$ in) ash splines. The grooves in the edge of the strips are machined with a 4mm ($^5/_{32}$ in) slotter attached to a router in a shop-made router table.

To allow for the double curvature of the strips the normal fence is replaced by a pair of guides; two pieces of hardboard clamped to the surface of the table prevent the curved strip rocking as it passes over the cutter.

Once the grooves have been machined the top edges of the strips are radiused with hand plane, file and sandpaper; the inside edges are chamfered by hand with a bullnose rabbet plane.

The corners left by planing may be quickly removed by the use of strips of sandpaper vigorously pulled back and forth over the edge, provided care is taken not

RIGHT: Simple router table rig for machining grooves into curved planks

PLANK WIDTH (For precision's sake an imperial conversion is not given)	
Centre plank	49mm
Intermediate planks	45mm
	41mm
	37mm
	33mm
Outside plank	29mm

to scratch the flat surface of the strip.

The scratch marks left on the radius are then removed by rubbing finer sandpaper parallel to the edge.

to follow the curve of the lid, *see photo 3*, with an allowance for spring-back estimated from the formula referred to in F&C 8.

The glued-up laminated strips are cleaned up and shaped as follows: a flexible steel ruler is used to mark one of the centre strip's straight edges just clear of any blobs of extruded glue; the waste is removed with a bandsaw and the edge cleaned up with a surface planer; the strip is then bandsawn and thicknessed to the correct width, the centre strip clamped on the lid frame, the next strip clamped next to it and the shape of the edge marked with a pair of dividers, *see photo 4*.

This slightly convex edge is then bandsawn and planed by hand, the strip sawn to width with a bandsaw and fence and the second slightly convex edge planed by hand. The slight degree of concavity may be coped with by skewing the smoothing plane to reduce the effective length of its sole; the blade may also be extended slightly.

This procedure is repeated until the last strip is shaped. Allowance must then be made for the gap which not only provides for slight movement but is also part of the decorative treatment.

For how to join the strips, *see panel*.

Fixing planks

For strength the planks should

probably be screwed and dowelled, but I wanted a clean look to the top so decided to rely on PVA glue, having first waxed the exposed surfaces of the insides.

For the method of clamping the planks to the frame, *see photo 5*. The slight transverse movement of the planks due to change of humidity is probably accommodated by the creep properties of PVA, particularly as the glue line is thicker towards the edges of the strip. After four years the glue is still holding.

The frame and strips are lipped with 6mm ($^1/_4$in) ash cut from the middle of the board from which the piece is made, and allowing the figure to follow the curve of the lid.

The bottom of the lip is hollowed with a router and glued to the frame to leave a recess which enables the lid to be opened with the fingers.

The lip on the back is continued around the rear of the frame and finishes at both sides of the hinges, *see photo 6*. The corners of the lips are mitred and glued in place with Cascamite.

The tops of the lipping are trimmed flush with the strips and the edges radiused in the same way as the strips described above. The lid is attached to the carcass with 3in brass butt hinges recessed with a router. ▪

LEFT: Sycamore bed with burr elm veneer detail

Suite dreams

Mark Griffiths exploits the biscuit jointer in making a set of bedroom furniture for the young lady of a client's house

ABOVE: Wardrobe with turned columns, and dressing table to match

'M ONE Of those makers who is always grumbling about a client's restrictive design preference, but in reality can only be at all creative when challenged by a close deadline, tight budget or dictated style brief.

In this case the clients allowed me the hellish task of answering the design questions, and permitted me weeks in which to wrack my brain for ideas.

I was finally rescued when my customers whipped my ideas into something visually interesting that suited their desire for a bedroom suite for a young girl, incorporating a wardrobe, chest of drawers, writing table, wall-mounted bedside table and bed, with a second pull-out mattress for a guest.

Timber choice

Sycamore (*Acer pseudoplatanus*) was chosen because this clean and bright timber looks sensational when turned into columns. The creaminess of the sycamore is contrasted with a burr elm (*Ulmus sp*) inlay strip, its fussy red-brown pattern making an ideal foil.

The burr inlay runs across the front of the bed – hiding the join of the guest bed's pull-out front – down the front of the wardrobe –

concealing the door join gap – down the centre of the drawer fronts to match the wardrobe and as a divider between the two small drawers on the writing table.

The bed is framed in 18mm, 9mm and 6mm MDF, and 25mm blockboard, relevant parts – like doors, drawers and tops – being lipped with solid sycamore.

Tracking device

To keep track of cut components I adopt a letter code which is jotted against each item on the cutting list and onto each part, together with the grain direction of the veneer to be laid and any other instructions.

White chalk is used because strong pencil markings can show through light veneers when sanded.

When the veneering is completed – I use a local firm with a large hot press for this unless the area to be covered is small enough to be hand-veneered quickly – the boards are belt-sanded with 120 grit paper on a four-inch hand-held machine. Each component is then cut to size and stacked in its relevant pile.

Because construction of the wardrobe, table and chest of

ABOVE: This chest of drawers uses metal runners

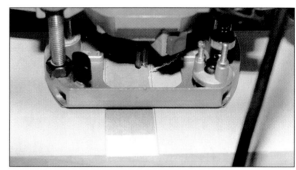

ABOVE: Rebate for the burr elm detailing to the drawer fronts is routed freehand, the edges trimmed with a chisel

ABOVE: The table is built from the top – note suspended centre drawer runner assembly

drawers is quite similar, I worked through these at the same time, leaving the bed until last.

The first, and most important, stage in this kind of carcass work is marking out the construction lines and biscuit locations. For this task I always reach for my invaluable metre steel rule and roofing square, using the old technique of marking the carcass sides 'TR' (top right) or 'TL' (top left) on the outside top corner of the job's front edge.

For simple carcass construction like this the biscuit jointer is king; and with the setting out complete it can be unleashed; quick, simple and accurate – however did we manage without them?

An 8mm, ^{5}/16in groove is routed into each component to take a 6mm MDF back. This is inset by 19mm, ^{3}/4in to allow for scribing to the skirting boards and uneven walls.

The tops and bases of the carcasses have their front corners bandsawed to fit around the turned columns.

Turnings

For uniformity, a local turner's copy lathe produced the 50mm, 2in turned columns for the fronts of the wardrobe and chest of drawers, plus the table legs and arms of the bed.

The turnings are dowelled onto the carcass uprights. To provide a firm seating, the front edges of the carcasses are routed using a 19mm, ^{3}/4in core box cutter.

Marking out for dowels on a cylinder is tricky, so they are held in a U-section holding box to provide a straight edge for the marking gauge. Small panel pins are then tapped halfway in along the marked line at 100mm, 4in intervals; snip off their heads and offer the turnings up to the carcasses, administering a sharp clout with a rubber mallet to transfer the dowel positions for drilling.

The wardrobe doors are hung on a 40mm, 1^5/8in strip which has a routed housing edge, fitted to the carcass' sides and their turnings.

Both carcasses are then dry-jointed together, checked for square and correct fit, sanded, glued and assembled.

Plinths

Plinths for the wardrobe and chest are made up from 20 by 60mm, ^{3}/4 by 2^3/8in solid sycamore with a routed 8mm, ^{5}/16in cove moulding. This is mitred to fit the underside of each unit, extending

"I suppose some people would spend a few hours making a jig on which the router would perform this operation with no risk of cutting over the marked lines, but then what's life without a few risks?"

6mm, ^{1}/4in beyond the columns, and fixed with counterbored screws.

Below this, cross-grain veneered blockboard is fitted at right angles, secured with glue blocks.

The top of the chest of drawers is simply fixed into place by screwing through the top rails that have been biscuited to the front and back of the carcass. The wardrobe top is a dummy to match the chest, and consists of lengths of 20 by 50mm, ^{3}/4 by 2in solid maple (*Acer saccharum*) mitred at the corners and screwed into position.

Writing table

Being veneered MDF, the writing table top can be structural, ➤

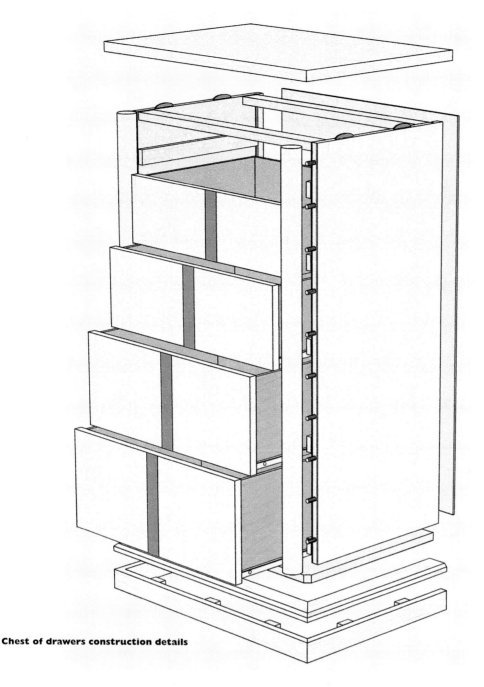

Chest of drawers construction details

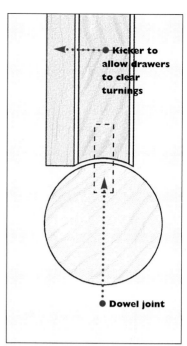

Chest of drawers construction details

holding the framework square, so must be biscuited into position.

The legs are dowelled onto the side and back rails in the same fashion as the column-to-carcass joints. This produces a three-sided framework which can simply be upended onto the underside of the table top for biscuit positions to be marked – once again demonstrating the unmatched simplicity of the biscuit jointer.

Drawer runners and kickers are also biscuited, the centre burr-veneered capping being fixed to the front of the suspended divider/runner assembly.

The drawers are dovetailed boxes are of solid oak (*Quercus sp*), on the front edges of which a 10mm, $^3/_8$in lipping is glued and shaped to fit around the curve of the leg.

The drawer fronts are hand-veneered in cross-grain sycamore.

Chest drawers

The chest drawers are fitted on metal runners, so require a different construction method. The drawer boxes are biscuited together, the bases fitted into slips – again jointed to the sides using '0' biscuits.

The runners are mounted on 16mm, $^5/_8$in packing strips fixed to the sides of the carcass to clear the protruding side turnings.

With the drawer boxes fitted and sitting squarely to the front of the carcass, the drawer fronts can be cut to size and the edges routed to fit around the turnings.

Each drawer front is then biscuited to its corresponding drawer box. With all the drawers

in position a 40mm, $1^5/_8$in wide strip is marked down the centre, first in pencil, and then, when satisfied that these lines run correctly through the drawer fronts, with a craft knife. This provides a guide for freehand routing of a rebate to take the burr elm inlay.

A 4mm, $^5/_{32}$in cut is made as close to the scored line as possible, leaving just a small amount to be cleaned away with a chisel.

Veneer inlay

I ruled out the use of a router fence along the edge of each drawer front because it is important that the veneer strip runs exactly in line through each drawer. I suppose I could have spent a few hours making a jig on which the router would perform this operation with no danger of cutting over the marked lines, but then what's life without a few risks?

Masking tape is laid up tight to the side of the exposed MDF, and the first of two coats of contact adhesive is applied. The burr elm strips can be cut to fit and spread with contact adhesive while waiting for the first coat to dry. Apply the second coat to the rebate.

The veneer strips are then carefully laid into position, placing one long edge down first, slowly folding the rest over into

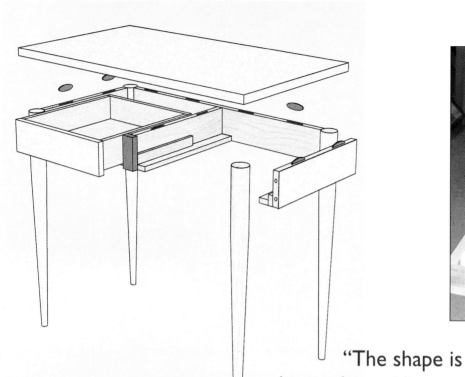

"The shape is cut out using a jigsaw, this tool providing greater control than that obtained from two blokes on a bandsaw"

the rebate and gently rubbing down with the flat end of a Warrington pattern hammer.

The veneer is finished with a cabinet scraper, made to fit the width of the rebate, and finally with abrasive paper.

Wardrobe doors

The inlay strip may be created more easily on the wardrobe doors. One is made 40mm, $^5/_{32}$in wider than the other, and then both are hung to the carcass with three $2^1/_2$in butt hinges each. When the doors have been shot in the wider one can be routed along its inner front edge to a depth of 4mm, $^5/_{32}$in and width of 40mm, $1^5/_8$.

The veneer strip is laid as before, and with that detail completed the doors and drawers can be given their final sanding.

The bed

The back and sides of the bed are made in 25mm block board, again veneered in sycamore. The back is cut square to size, and half of the curved shape plotted out on a length of hardboard. The curve is cut out on the bandsaw and cleaned up with a spokeshave to ensure a sweeping curve.

This is used as a template, mirrored, for the serpentine shape of the back. The back was cut out using a jigsaw, this tool providing greater control than

that obtained with two blokes on a bandsaw.

The cut edge is smoothed with a spokeshave, and the gaps in the blockboard filled with a strong two-part filler. A final sanding with 120 grit paper is followed by contact adhesive and a long-grain strip of sycamore veneer.

Solid sycamore end caps are fixed to each edge of the back using a double line of offset biscuits. These give strength to a section which takes the bed sides' fixing bolts.

Turnings

Solid sycamore turnings run along the top edge of each side, set off-centre to create a roll-over effect, thus lending the bed the look of a large sofa. This is achieved by making a housing box into which the sycamore turning can be secured.

Drill three dowel holes through the ends of the box, matching them with holes in the end of each turning, these being used to locate the headboard and fixings for the front posts. With the turning secured in the box, set up the router to produce a 27 mm, $1^1/_8$in wide 20mm, $^3/_4$in deep rebate to take the blockboard bed sides; these are then marked out with dowel pins and doweled into place as before.

The resultant cross-section of the ends can now be used as a

ABOVE: The trundle bed is pulled out like a drawer

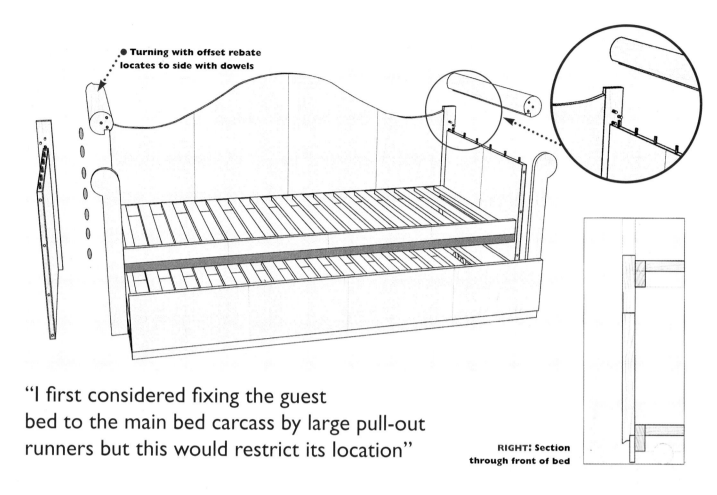

● **Turning with offset rebate locates to side with dowels**

RIGHT: Section through front of bed

"I first considered fixing the guest bed to the main bed carcass by large pull-out runners but this would restrict its location"

template for the front post, which are cut from 25mm, 1in solid sycamore selected for good grain pattern.

The posts are made with a 10mm, ³⁄₈in overhang around the turning and 25mm, 1in each side of the blockboard ends. After shaping and sanding, these posts are glued into place using the dowel holes made in the turnings for location in the holding box, with extra ones along the edge of the blockboard.

BELOW:
Bed arms are routed out to take the sides

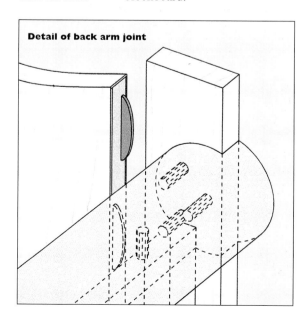

Detail of back arm joint

Rails

Again, the front rail is made up from 25mm, 1in blockboard, lipped in solid timber and veneered in cross-grain sycamore.

The lower 40mm, 1⁵⁄₈in of the rail is rebated and veneered in burr elm to match the other pieces. Housings routed into the inside ends take coach bolt fixings.

The front of the bed is made of two sections, the front rail being bolted to each of the ends to give the framework strength. The lower section is the pull-out front of the lower guest bed.

This front is also veneered in cross-grain sycamore, and has a 60mm, 2³⁄₈in solid plinth which is set back 15mm, ⁵⁄₈in. Together with a routed coving cut on the back of the bottom edge of the pull-out front, this acts as a finger hold when drawing out the guest bed, *see panel*.

Base

Ash (*Fraxinus sp*) is an excellent timber for bed and seating construction where strength and flexibility are needed.

The main bed base comprises 20 by 60mm, ³⁄₄ by 2³⁄₈in ash slats, fixed into 40 by 60mm, 1⁵⁄₈ by 2³⁄₈in rails running along the back and front rail, set down

20mm, ³⁄₄in from the top of the front rail to take the bed mattress. The slats are fixed with one screw in each end, the first and last having a screw batten biscuited along their lengths which is screwed to each side, thus providing a little extra carcass strength.

Bedside shelf

A small bedside shelf is simply made from a 300 by 200mm, 12 by 8in piece lipped and veneered in sycamore, with a C-shaped fixing bracket cut from 25mm, 1in solid sycamore attached underneath.

All the pieces may now be disassembled and finished with a hard-wearing cellulose lacquer before re-assembly on site – in my case with the direction of young Holly, the delighted new owner. ▪

BELOW: End cappings are joined with a double row of staggered biscuits

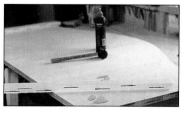

● **WILLIAM J. KIRKBRIGHT** studied at Brunel College, Bristol between 1992 and 1993, gaining a City and Guilds Furniture Craft Certificate. He returned to his native Tyne and Wear to set up a small workshop producing fine furniture, sometimes featuring carving and turning, and interior joinery. He also undertakes some restoration commissions and can be contacted on 0191 4166950.

LEFT: Based on a Sheraton design, this bonheur du jour is made from American walnut

BELOW: The writing surface open, supported on lopers

Skills ancient and

William Kirkbright looks to Sheraton for this bonheur du jour

TO COMPLETE my City and Guilds Furniture Craft Certificate I was required to produce a fine piece by means of a variety of traditional and modern cabinetmaking techniques. Before looking at possible designs, however, I decided that whatever piece was chosen it would be made in American black walnut (*Juglans nigra*), it would incorporate some woodcarving and would be presented to my wife.

While looking for suitable ideas I discovered in Sheraton's *The Cabinet Maker's and Upholsterer's Drawing Book* a design for a lady's small writing table. From this finding came the idea of producing an individual interpretation of a traditional piece of fine furniture,

incorporating the three criteria stated above.

After extensive research, including visits to London's Victoria and Albert Museum and many sketches and drawings, I settled on a design of correct proportions which requires the utilisation of both traditional and modern skills.

Sub-assemblies

The work is organised into three sections – table underframe, table top and cabinet.

The polishing, *see panel*, is the penultimate operation, the laying of the leather skiver being left until last.

Table underframe

Joint the back, sides and front drawer rails to the legs – still

square at this stage – using mortise and tenons and lap dovetails, *see illustration*. Complete the jointing of the main components by adding the small upright rails between the lower and top drawer rails with twin stub tenons.

Fit the drawer runners and kickers – I used reclaimed oak (*Quercus sp*) for its wear resistance. Both components are stub tenoned into the back edges of the drawer rails, the drawer runners being fitted first, and the loper and drawer guides being added before the kickers are secured.

Tapered legs

There are many methods of tapering legs; I use a technique involving the surface planer. A stop is G-clamped to the infeed

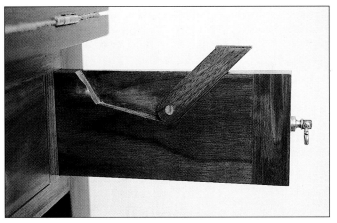

ABOVE: Detail of the loper's peg – an alternative approach is to make the front of the loper full-height, notching out the top drawer rail to accommodate it when closed

ABOVE: The main drawer's bottom is in two parts, grooved into a central muntin

"Two pigeonholes are attached with glue and the middle one acts as the front for a pull-out candle slide – although a secret drawer may be preferred"

modern

ABOVE: Drawers are hand dovetailed with oak linings, the bottoms are fitted with slips

table so that the distance from stop to the planer knives is just less than the length of the taper required.

To produce the taper, place the foot of the leg against the stop and, sliding the leg against the planer fence in an arc, carefully lower it onto the moving knife block. Move the leg over the planer in the usual way, transferring pressure to the outfeed table as the centre of the leg passes the half-way point. Take off about 1.5mm ($^{1}/_{16}$in) on each pass until the required taper is achieved, but leave 0.5 mm ($^{1}/_{64}$in) full for cleaning up afterwards by hand.

Editor's note: It will be obvious that this is a potentially dangerous procedure. To ensure that your fingers stay well away from the knives, use a push stick. A safer technique is to make a simple tapered jig for use in the thicknesser.

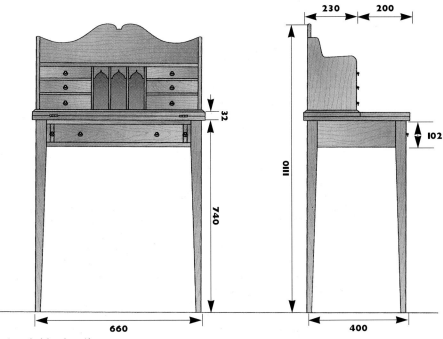

▶ **Front and side elevations**

230   200

32

102

1110

740

660

400

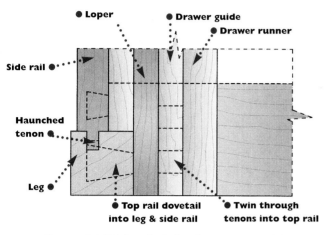

● Loper
● Drawer guide
● Drawer runner
Side rail ●
Haunched tenon ●
Leg ●
● Top rail dovetail into leg & side rail
● Twin through tenons into top rail

Corner detail (plan view) showing arrangement for loper pockets

> "The choice of veneer for the table top in preference to solid walnut enabled another skill to be exercised"

Underframe assembly
Before the underframe is glued up – and in preparation for securing the top – drill screw clearance holes in the top drawer rail and the drawer kickers, and pockets for screw-fixing through the back rail.

After sanding all inside faces the underframe is now ready for assembly in sequence. The side rails are glued to the legs to produce two ends; when dry these are joined by adding the back rail and lower drawer rail.

Using G cramps, complete the assembly by adding the two small drawer muntins and the top

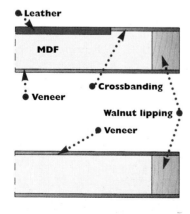

● Leather
MDF
● Crossbanding
● Veneer
Walnut lipping ●
● Veneer

Sections showing lipping, veneer and leather skiver

drawer rail, ensuring that both top and bottom drawer rails are perfectly aligned.

Lopers
The folding flap of the table top necessitates the fitting of lopers into the underframe; due to the thickness of the top drawer rail, a peg is added to make up the difference in height.

Begin by fitting an end cleat to the loper with a stub tenon, then obtain a good fit in its channel in the underframe assembly. Cut the recess for the peg with a router, cleaning up with a sharp chisel.

Fix the peg into position using a brass screw, or glue in a rivet, but remember to wax the underside of the peg first to prevent any excess glue from sticking to it.

With the peg secure add a small piece of baize to its top edge to prevent any scratches or blemishes to the decorative face veneer of the extended folding flap.

Complete the loper by fixing a stop to its inside face, remembering to allow for the thickness of the drawer guide below. A piece of baize could also be added to the end of the stop as a finishing touch.

Table top
The choice of veneer for the table top in preference to solid walnut enables another skill to be exercised. MDF is used as the substrate due to its stability. Three pieces are required, all lipped with 10mm (3/8in) thick American walnut and edge jointed with biscuits, or a loose tongue could be used if preferred.

The base section of the assembly receives walnut backing veneer. The face side veneer covers only the area equivalent to the underside of the top section which sits above it. The top section is then glued and screwed to the base.

The folding flap features decorative acanthus leaves in marquetry.

All three sections are veneered using Cascamite adhesive; I cold pressed them in a platen press, but a home-made caul assembly or traditional hammer veneering could also be used successfully.

Brass back flap hinges fitted slightly below the surface of the MDF join the folding flap to the base. Fill with chemical metal and sand level to avoid the possibility of the screw heads

ever protruding through the leather.

Complete the table top assembly by adding the walnut cross banding and the moulded frame, which is secured to the top section with screws.

Cabinet construction
Begin by jointing the cabinet base to the two sides with lapped dovetails; fit the top into stopped housings, which are produced using a router. All dividers are housed, except the outer left and right pigeon hole uprights, which are stub tenoned to provide extra rigidity.

With the sides still square, rout

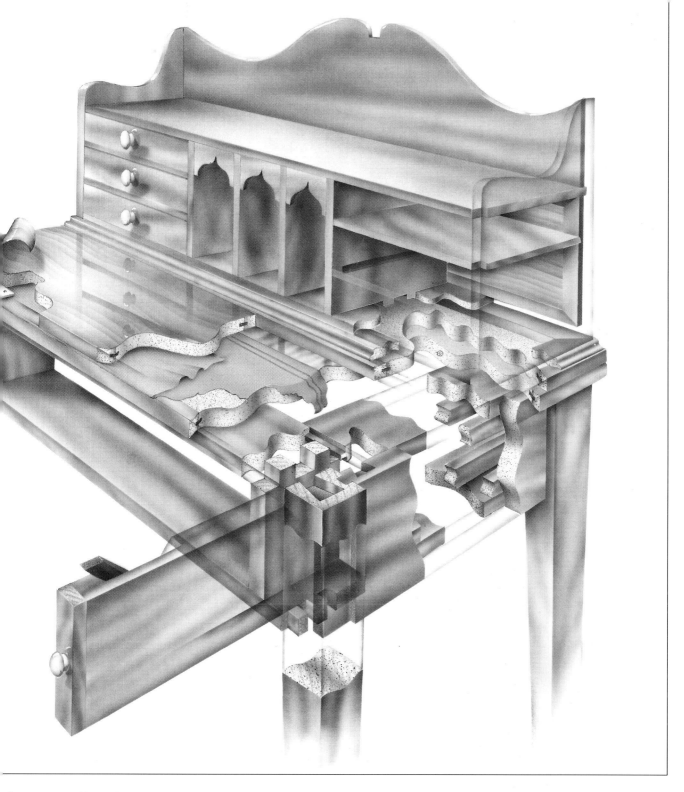

the grooves which will accept the carved back panel. Tape the sides' inside faces together and cut to shape on a bandsaw, cleaning up afterwards with a spokeshave and scraper.

The back of the cabinet is made up from two sections, the base being of frame and panel construction to avoid shrinkage.

Grooves are run on all inside edges of the frame and stub tenons made to suit these. Two panels are made, polished and added to complete this sub-assembly which can now be glued together and put to one side.

Begin the second section by cutting the tongues in the left and right edges, then cut the panel to shape. After carving, the panel should be polished prior to assembly.

Cabinet assembly

For convenience of clean-up and access, all inside faces are polished before assembly as follows:

1. Glue the pigeonhole dividers into their relevant mortises and housings in the cabinet base and top; positioning the sides assists in keeping the unit square during cramping;

2. When these are dry, glue the ➤

LEFT: Detail of the panelled part of the back

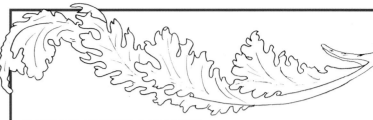

FINISHING

WHILE CONSIDERING possible finishes, I decided that a natural colour and mellow sheen would best complement the appearance of the piece.

With no stain used, the grain is treated with a pigment-based filler, left to dry thoroughly, then bodied up with white polish.

This is cut back with 0000 grade wire wool; two coats of clear paste wax are applied and buffed to produce an eggshell sheen.

> "I decided that a natural colour and mellow sheen would be required to complement the appearance of the piece"

base and top to the sides; shaped cramping blocks enable even, downward pressure to be applied;

3. Glue the drawer dividers and slide them into position;

4. Secure the frame and panelled back;

5. Complete the assembly by placing the carved back panel into position, securing with shaped cramping blocks and sash cramps.

The shaped pigeonhole fronts are now fitted. Two are attached with glue and the middle one acts as the front for a pull-out candle slide – although a secret drawer may be preferred.

Drawers

The drawers are constructed in traditional style with hand-cut dovetails. I chose reclaimed quarter-sawn oak for all sides and backs as it is fairly stable; flat-sawn stock was employed for bases.

FAR RIGHT: The frieze of the top carcass contains a candle slide

The 6mm (1/4in) sides require drawer slips – which are grooved with a specifically made router jig – The drawers are completed with the addition of period brass handles.

Leather skiver

The production of a 25mm (1in) wide chamfer alongside all four edges of the crossbanding prepares the table top for the leather skiver. This is taken to a depth equivalent to the thickness of the leather.

Apply a heavy scalpel to

DECORATIVE TOUCH

TO EXECUTE the carving detail, begin by drawing a vertical and horizontal centre line onto both the back panel and a piece of tracing paper.

Set a marking gauge to 6mm (^{1}/$_4$in) and gouge a line from all four edges to create the carving depth. After tracing the design, position the tracing paper onto the panel, fixing it with pins so that the centre lines coincide.

Place carbon paper between the panel and tracing paper, and transfer the design onto the wood.

The wood is cut away around the design to form the ground. With a v-tool, cut a trench about 3mm (^{1}/$_8$in) from the outline. Remove the waste wood to the 6mm (^{1}/$_4$in) depth, working the gouge from the gauge line to the v-trench. Level off any ridges with a No. 3 gouge; if preferred, a router could be employed for this operation, 0.5mm (^{1}/$_{32}$in) being allowed for cleaning up with a gouge.

The design is set in – across the grain first – by holding suitable tools perpendicular to the outline of the design and hammering them in to the 6mm, ^{1}/$_4$in depth.

ABOVE: Carving to back

The design is enlivened by modelling with relevant tools, and is completed by undercutting so that it stands out from the panel.

A shoe brush is rubbed over the carving to brighten it before polishing prior to assembly.

achieve a 3mm (1/8in) deep groove at the edge of the crossbanding for use when laying the leather, *see below.*

Gluing on a 50mm (2in) wide strip of hessian should overcome stress on the leather where the main table top and extending flap join.

To glue the skiver, prepare some starch wallpaper paste and spread evenly onto the surface. Gently place the leather in position, smoothing it down from the centre outwards to ensure that all creases are removed.

Slots are cut around the hinged knuckles before the leather can

be trimmed with a scalpel, running the blade in the groove prepared earlier.

When the glue has dried, the completed piece can be set up by securing the table top to the underframe and the cabinet to the table top with brass screws. ◼

Curved and fumed

Kevin Ley thanks French foresight for providing the timber for this fumed oak table

I N THE DISTANT past the French were required by law to plant two oaks for every one they cut down, so ensuring plentiful future supplies for warships. This exercise in forward planning resulted in many of the trees being planted close together in stands, a method which encourages tall straight growth with a clean bole.

With warships now built from steel, furniture-makers can take advantage of this good husbandry to reap the benefits, in this case some very nice quarter-sawn French oak (*Quercus robur*).

The wood is mild, clean and straight-grained, with a good figure and consistent colour. The minimum available board thickness is generally 28mm (1 $^1/_8$in), giving scope for thicker finished pieces. I took advantage of this for the top of the table.

> "Because I have an aversion to spending time making a jig for what is essentially a small one-off job, I did it by hand"

Oak courtesy of French law, design from the Shakers

● On leaving the RAF in 1987 KEVIN LEY set to turning his hobby into a commercial proposition. The former squadron leader designs and makes bespoke furniture from his cottage and workshop in Shropshire.

Design

My client, who specified the height and diameter of the top, is particularly fond of fumed oak and wanted a Shaker influence in the piece.

The starting point for the design was a Shaker round stand on which candles would have been placed; this would more usually have had double arc tapered legs, but we decided on the double-curved or serpentine legs shown here.

The column profile takes on a soft curve in keeping with the leg shape.

The top has a substantial 22mm ($^7/_8$in) section to provide strength, the edge being bevelled down to 16mm ($^5/_8$in) to maintain the delicate look.

The edges of the top and legs are rounded over to improve the highlights of the oiled finish and generally enhance the look and feel of the piece.

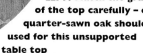

LEFT: Match the grain of the top carefully – only quarter-sawn oak should be used for this unsupported table top

Top

Select the best pieces of wood for the top and match them carefully, as this surface will be the one on which the piece is judged. I used pieces from the same board to ensure even colour and flowing pattern of grain and figure, these factors being especially important when fuming.

Check that the pieces are truly quarter-sawn, with the grain running vertically through the thickness of the board, to ensure stability and minimum future movement.

After matching, plane the edges slightly hollow at the centre so that the ends pull up tight when clamped. Check that the top is flat with a straight edge, and leave to set.

Cut the brace to size, curving the ends to follow the top edge. Drill a 25mm (1in) hole in the centre to take the turned end of the column.

Cutting bevels

The bevels on the underside of the top and the brace can either be cut on the lathe – if a big enough example is available – or by using jigs on standing machines or even the router.

My lathe is not large enough and, because I have an aversion ➤

TOP: Underside of table showing brace connecting the column to the top

"I drew the leg freehand in chalk until I was happy with the shape and curves, pencilled it in, then cut it out as a pattern"

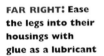

FAR RIGHT: Ease the legs into their housings with glue as a lubricant

RIGHT: Routing the dovetail housings while the column is mounted on the lathe, using a simple jig

to spending time making a jig for what is essentially a small one-off job, I did this by hand. Mark the width and depth of the bevel, sharpen up the smoothing plane, clamp the work to the bench and, with a coarseish but comfortable set to the plane, remove the bulk of the waste. When close to the lines, re-sharpen and set the plane, finishing to the line – much more satisfying than all that noise and dust!

To finish off, round over the top edge of the top to 6mm (¹/₄in) radius with the router and soften the bottom edge with a sanding block.

Brace preparation
Position the brace on the underside of the top with the grain running at right angles. Prepare four slots – or oversized holes with spacing washers to allow for movement – for the screws.

As this wood was kiln-dried quarter-sawn, and the diameter of the top is quite small, the amount of movement is also likely to be minimal.

In this case I used a hole countersunk from each side; this provides a neat result with enough purchase to hold the top down, and allows some side-to-side movement.

Put the brace aside for later fitting to the column.

Column
Cut the column blank to size and turn it to shape – a gentle tapering curve from top to bottom looks less severe than a straight taper and is more compatible with the double curved legs.

LEVELLING THE LEGS

WHILE A three-legged table will always have all its legs on the ground and won't rock, it is more difficult to level. The best way is to stand it on a known level surface – I keep a 6ft by 4ft piece of 1in MDF, levelled as a reference surface, on the workshop floor – and check with a spirit level.

Wedge up one or two feet as necessary to achieve the level, and adjust until only one foot is wedged to retain the level, reducing the other two feet by that amount.

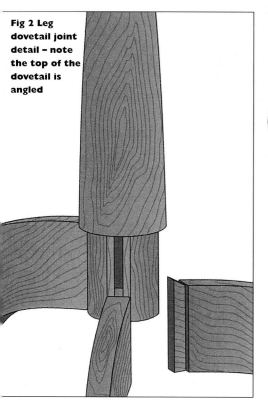

Fig 2 Leg dovetail joint detail – note the top of the dovetail is angled

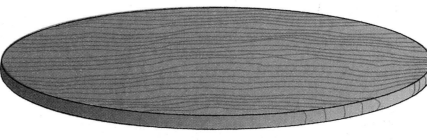

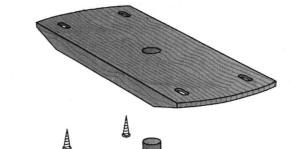

"This joint is a bit fiddly to achieve, but a little cautious practice on pieces of scrap helps avoid disaster so make haste slowly!"

The fixing peg on the top is best finished with a sizing tool to ensure a good all-round fit. Using the sizing tool on the leg recess as well achieves a good straight line for the leg joints.

Leg joints

The running dovetail housing for the legs is most easily cut while the column is still on the lathe. For this I think it is worthwhile making a simple jig – I have had full value out of mine!

The precise arrangement depends on lathe and router, but the principle is a fixed stand attached to the lathe, supporting a sliding table to which the router is attached. This enables a housing groove to be cut in the leg recess.

Use of a reference point or indexing on the lathe enables work to be turned through 120° twice to make the three housings.

To achieve a dovetail housing first remove most of the waste with a smaller straight cutter before a final pass with a 13mm

($^1/2$in) dovetail cutter. This avoids overloading the router, and/or breaking the dovetail cutter – the whole dovetail shape must be cut in one pass; the undercut does not allow a number of shallow passes to be made.

The resulting housings, 13mm wide at the bottom of the cut by 13mm deep, could be cut by hand with a fine tenon saw and finished with a chisel, but they would take very careful marking out, great care, a long time and are unlikely to be as accurate as those cut with the router.

Legs

Cut a piece of hardboard 270mm (10$^1/2$in) wide by 260mm (10in) high and mark the outline of the leg on it through the diagonal – this results in the tenon end for the running dovetail being at right angles to the base of the foot; be sure to allow for the dovetail tenon on the width.

RIGHT: **Fig 1 Only six components make this table**

I drew the leg freehand in chalk until I was happy with the shape and curves, pencilled it in, then cut it out as a pattern.

Cut out three legs from 19mm ($^3/4$in) stock, ensuring the grain direction runs at 45° top to bottom. This gives maximum strength by avoiding short grain anywhere. Round over the edges ➤

"Do not let any oil build up on the surface as it will quickly look syrupy and spoil the effect – less is best"

ABOVE: The desired effect

of the legs to a 6mm ($^{1}/_{4}$in) radius, and finish.

Dovetail tenon

To fit the legs to the column either the shoulders of the leg tenons must be undercut to allow for the curve of the column or the column's face must be flattened with a sharp chisel. I find the latter much easier.

A $^{3}/_{4}$in chisel centred over the housing should give the exact width of face required. This joint is a bit fiddly to achieve, but a little cautious practice on pieces of scrap helps avoid disaster, so make haste slowly!

With the dovetail cutter that was used for the housing, and the router mounted on its table, set the fence so that each side of the leg tenon end can be run against it to cut each side of the tenon.

This is not as difficult to set up as might be thought – perform test runs to check fit by using some scraps of the stock from which the legs were cut. In the absence of a router table, the router can, with extreme care, be used hand-held with its side

fence on the leg, this being held in a vice.

The top of the dovetail should be angled to match the sides; fitting the housing end left by the rotary dovetail cutter, *see illustration*.

Assembly

Apply glue to the inside of the dovetail housing and, using the glue as a lubricant, slide the legs into position. Make sure they are pushed tightly home, and leave to set.

Glue and fit the central hole in the brace over the peg on the column; pull down and strengthen the joint by countersinking two $1^{1}/_{2}$in No. 8 screws through the brace, down into the column, either side of and parallel to the peg. Leave to set.

Lastly, with the top face down on a soft, padded surface, screw the brace to the top through the prepared holes.

Finishing

All pieces should be finished and sanded as far as possible before assembly. Before fuming, all

surplus glue must be cleaned off, particularly from around the joints. Check the whole piece carefully for marks, blemishes, rough spots, raised grain etc.

Prepare a polythene tent to fit over the table, ensuring that it is clear of all surfaces of the table, and place about 5fl oz of 880 ammonia in a container inside. If in a reasonably warm place, leave overnight, if cold, leave for 48 hours.

Oiling really suits oak. Apply a liberal coat, refreshing it as necessary until it will take no more; wipe off all surplus, buff and leave to dry in a warm, dry place for 24 hours.

Give a further light coat every 24 hours until the desired effect is achieved; four or five coats are usually enough. Do not let any oil build up on the surface as it will quickly look syrupy and spoil the effect – less is best.

Conclusion

Though a relatively simple piece with only six components and six joints, it is interesting, demanding and rewarding to make.

The fumed and oiled oak is resilient and ages well. The inevitable marks and bruises that will occur can be 'oiled in' to give real character with time and tender loving care!

School report

Andrew Skelton on building education and quality into budget-priced shelving

WELL MADE AND designed objects ought to be part of everyday life. I'm not talking about high points of craftsmanship or fabulous and expensive items, but about the ordinary, though regrettably scarcely seen; a neatly painted window frame, tidily pointed brickwork and a beautiful stone wall spring to mind.

Woodworkers, of course, are excited by the quality of furniture and joinery, by the sort of piece that begs examination – when no-one is looking – on hands and knees. This sort of work is distinguished by the fact that the maker has cared, revealed perhaps in the selection of a fine piece of oak (*Quercus robur*) or attention to a detail that lifts the whole piece.

When I first started out as a woodworker I worked in rural Kent; there I would see woodwork in the local church and then recognise the hand of the same anonymous maker in window frames and doors throughout the village.

Spurred on by reading the writings of William Morris who, more than a century ago, thundered about the lack of quality in everyday goods, I wanted to be part of this tradition of good workmanship, not in any egocentric way but as part of a continuing community of craftsmen.

Time went on, and both necessity and chance led mercifully along roads never thought of; the notion that I would leave behind me a village of beautifully crafted woodwork has not come to fruition – not that I am advocating losing sight of ideals...

Over the years I have been fortunate that much of my work has been for public buildings and gardens, as this is the type of work that I enjoy most. I was delighted, then, when the local primary school at which I have three children asked me to make some shelves.

Cost restriction

Furniture design is about working within practical restraints; the size of the room, the limitations of the material, the techniques of construction, ergonomics and anthropometrics.

> "Whichever adjustable shelf support system is chosen the holes will never be in the right place"

But cost should come at the top of the list, for this affects all subsequent decisions. Whether the cost is unrestricted, restricted, severely restricted or, as in this case, very severely restricted, has profound implications for the design.

I feel that I have failed as a designer when I have to say "I can't look at it for that amount of money". So these shelves had to fit in a space, hold a certain number of books and be made to a price.

My design uses a minimum amount of material and a quick, conventional form of construction. The shelves will not help William Morris to lie peacefully in his grave, but I hope that they show some thought and care.

The design

I have had wild and romantic ideas about furniture, and indeed buildings, for schools which could provide a visual and tactile library of materials and techniques. A small step in this direction is to use different timbers for the shelf lippings into which the names of the woods are carved. I realised later that these lippings provide a perfect use for those wild-grained and structurally unsound off-cuts that normally go into the stove.

Cost limitations prevented the further exploitation of educational ideas such as a design highlighting smell, texture, leaf shape, bark and growing pattern, all of which would ➤

● **ANDREW SKELTON** has been making high quality hardwood furniture for the past 15 years. He trained as an architect and says that furniture making is a natural progression from that discipline. He lives and works in the Derbyshire Peak District.

BELOW: PHOTO 1 – Cramping up lippings in multiples.

ABOVE: **PHOTO 2** – Routing mitres: cutter looks lethal but works well, note anti-spelch fence screwed to guide board.

ABOVE: **Photo 3** – Biscuiting uprights using scrap MDF as fence.

have given the pupils a knowledge and love of wood. The work of a sculptor-furniture maker like Tim Stead suggests what might be possible.

These shelves comprise three units which go either side and beneath an existing notice board and fit over a heating pipe, *see fig one*.

While this project was made for an individual situation, a simple box with adjustable shelves and a back to give rigidity, that can be neatly fitted to a wall, will serve many purposes. The following description concentrates on this basic unit.

These shelves had to fit on a wall which varied by about 20mm, ^{3}/4in. Thus the carcass is rebated by 6mm, ^{1}/4in for the back plus a 20mm, ^{3}/4in allowance for scribing to the wall, making the sides and top 26mm, 1in wider than the shelves.

Cutting MDF

MDF was chosen for its ease of use and ready-to-finish surface. Unless the shelves are to be fixed and screwed through the back they must be 25mm, 1in thick for spans of 600mm, 24in or more. This is to avoid sagging when the shelves are loaded.

Once the pieces are cut to width they can be left over length, the edges being carefully shot on the overhand planer for lipping. This job is cruel on the blades due to the abrasive nature of MDF, so it is wise to dedicate one area of the knives to it – but a perfect joint results.

Gluing lippings

The lippings are prepared a touch oversize and biscuit slots cut every 100mm, 4in or so. When gluing the lippings use an adhesive with a long open time – it seems to take ages to glue up biscuit slots – and cramp up the lipped shelves two or four at a time, arranging the pieces in the cramps lipping-to-lipping so that the width of the MDF distributes the pressure evenly, *see photo one*.

When the glue is set, clean the lippings flush with a sharp plane or belt sander and cut the pieces to length.

Cutting mitres

I can cut square ends adequately with my saw bench but long mitres never seem to be good enough, so I have taken to trimming them with a router. The 45° cutter capable of chamfering a 25mm, 1in board looks lethal but, run at a slow speed and taking off only a skim, mine handles very smoothly.

The cutter's guide bearing follows an MDF straight edge clamped to the underside of the piece being mitred. This straight edge should be about 30mm, 1^1/4in wider than the mitre at each side to allow a safe lead in,

FIG 1

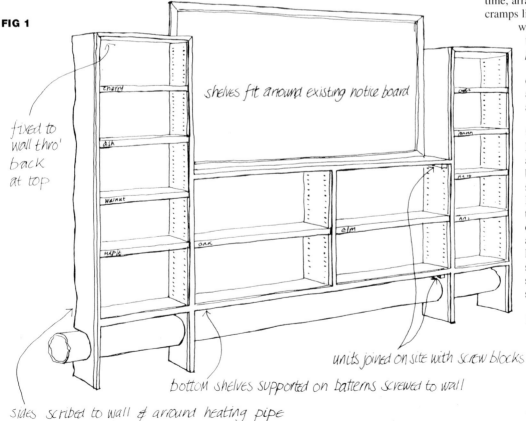

shelves fit around existing notice board

fixed to wall thro' back at top

cherry

ash

walnut

maple

oak

elm

units joined on site with screw blocks

bottom shelves supported on battens screwed to wall

sides scribed to wall & around heating pipe

nd a scrap piece screwed to
t prevents the lipping spelching
out at the end of the cut, *see photo
wo.*

Biscuit joints

The biscuit slots can now be cut.
Handle with care until the biscuited
outt joint can be strengthened by the
back as it is not very strong; two
ows of biscuits seem to give no
marked improvement.

Use a scrap of MDF marked with
the position of the biscuits clamped
o the uprights as a fence for
oiscuiting across these parts; the
same piece can be used to transfer
these positions to the fixed shelves,
ee photo three.

A mitred biscuit joint, on the other
hand, seems to be strong, but be sure
to set the biscuit jointer to cut
owards the inside of the mitre where
t has the most bulk. A mitre in
25mm, 1in material will take a No.
20 biscuit.

Chamfers

There are many methods of
supporting adjustable shelves,
rom drilling scores of holes to
using ready made systems –
whichever is chosen, the holes will
hever be in the right place! If using a
onk strip which is set flush with the
surface, rout the channels for it at
his stage. Next rout the rebate on the
back edge, and attend to the
chamfers.

These run through all the joints,
and the ends of the fixed shelves
and mitres are chamfered with a
chisel.

I chose to do this to emphasise the
intersections of the pieces and to
show clearly that some joints are at
90° and some at 45°; usual practice
would be to make the joining as
perfect and invisible as possible.

Staining lippings

This approach also allowed the
staining and finishing of each
component before assembly; the
giant size 'Danish shoulder' hides
any slight misalignment.

The lippings can be stained after
the edges and chamfers are cleaned
up. I used a water stain so it was
necessary to raise the grain and sand
back several times before
application.

To stain only the lippings leaving

the MDF clean, apply as carefully as
possible; when it is dry rout a
1.5mm, $^1/_{16}$in V-groove to clean up
the ragged edge, *see photo four.* With
all the joints masked the components
can be sprayed with a hard-wearing
lacquer.

Carcass assembly

The method of gluing up mitres used
here may seem extravagant but,
having gone to the trouble to achieve
good joints, it is worth spending a ➤

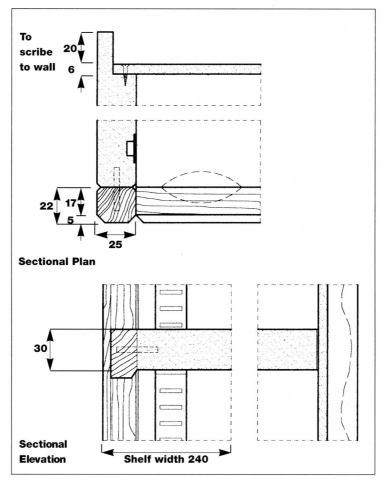

Sectional Plan

Sectional Elevation   ← **Shelf width 240** →

ABOVE: PHOTO 6 – Lower joint cramped with sash cramps and slightly curved blocks.

ABOVE: The finished shelves; short names are preferred!

little time on assembly.

Triangular blocks, glued and screwed to hardboard or thin MDF, are G-cramped tightly to the carcass. The mitres are drawn together with cramps applied to these blocks; in this way the pressure acts directly across the joints, *see photo five*.

The lower joint is cramped with sash cramps top and bottom, using slightly rounded blocks to apply pressure over the whole width. Glue can easily be wiped off the finished surfaces, another benefit of finishing before assembly.

The back is cut from 6mm MDF and, working on the principle of much modern joinery, lots of small fixings were used to spread the load and create a strong structure. No. 4 screws were inserted every 150mm, 6in or so – note that while No. 6 screws into the endgrain of 25mm MDF might work, No. 8s will almost certainly cause the material to delaminate.

Carving names

I am no carver and have only a few gouges picked up in second-hand shops, but I would recommend anyone to attempt carving the names. Calligraphy skills aren't necessary – the letters can be printed out from a computer at the appropriate size and traced through using carbon paper, or marked out using Letraset-type rub-down transfers.

At this point you will be glad to have chosen homely timbers with (short) names like oak and elm, rather than Papua New Guinea rosewood (*Dalbergia*).

PHOTOGRAPHY BY STEPHEN HEPWORTH

DUST PROTECTION

Cutting MDF is a heavy and unpleasant task, and precautions must be taken against the dust produced. MDF produces tiny, invisible dust particles when machined which bypass the body's defences. Together with the chemical content, which includes Formaldehyde, of the adhesive used in its manufacture this dust presents a serious health hazard, so dust protection capable of filtering sub-one micron particles must be worn. Budget dust masks do not qualify – use only those for which the makers provide specifications of protection levels, and for sustained use choose an air-fed respirator.

Remember that the dust remains suspended in the air for some time after machining.

High fidelity

Mike Cowie's exercise in construction features wooden full-extension runners to the drawers

RIGHT: Cabinet designed to accommodate hi-fi equipment

● **This hi-fi unit was presented to Sheffield Parkwood College in appreciation of my time spent there as a student learning the craft of furniture-making on a City & Guilds advanced course. It is being raffled to raise some much needed funds.**
The course run by Harry Sampson, assisted by Malcolm Herring, offers the opportunity to train or retrain, in the case of redundancy or retirement, in the production of handmade furniture, in a small though well equipped workshop.
For further information, contact Harry or Malcolm on 0114 260 2400.

THIS HI-FI CABINET was built as a stop-gap piece, and was originally intended to replace a chipboard creation that lives in my sitting room.

Made predominantly from American white oak (*Quercus alba*), of standard 20mm, $^{25}/_{32}$ in thickness, it was an exercise in overcoming various problems posed particularly by seeking to add refinement to drawers designed to be opened to their full length without strain.

Uniformity of size of carcass, plinth, shelves, drawer fronts, frame and panel doors aided the speed at which this cabinet could be completed.

The basic dimensions were governed by the available wood being in 5ft lengths. This was planed up to 20.5mm, $^{13}/_{16}$ in and selected for jointing to the necessary widths.

Preparation

Here the Plano glue press, a speculative buy when I could afford such things, does an excellent job with minimal fuss, and is particularly useful in cramped conditions. Sash cramps would do the job, but be careful to alternate them on both sides of the panel being glued, to avoid bowing under uneven pressure. When dry, clean up and flatten the boards selected for the carcass.

Square off one edge of each panel to use as a datum for marking the position of the mitres, and mark on the shelf locations. Measure and mark on one side, then transfer directly to the opposite side to avoid inaccuracy; at least then if the measure is wrong both sides are wrong in the right place!

Cutting mitres

I was fortunate in that a dimension saw was available to cut the long mitres. The same result can be achieved with a portable saw, batten and a mitre shooting board, though not as fast! Andrew Skelton uses a router with a large chamfer cutter to good effect for this job, *see School shelves, F&C issue 2*.

The cut mitres are biscuit jointed; this not only strengthens the joint, it also acts as an aid to gluing up by providing a positive location. Decorative dovetails added as a feature on the side panels can now be marked and cut.

Until expediency asserted itself, I had intended that a small dovetailed fillet of contrasting wood should be slid in place for these; for reasons too boring to go into here mahogany wood filler had to be used, giving a surprisingly good appearance.

"Measure and mark on one side, then transfer directly to the mating side to avoid inaccuracy; at least then if the measure is wrong both sides are wrong in the right place!"

ABOVE: Angled joint of door is a bridle joint

Carcass assembly

A stepped housing can now be routed out for the fixed shelf; the shelf also incorporates through tenons to help strengthen the carcass. A shoulder is cut at the front of the shelf for neatness; mark the mortises directly from the tenons, drill a pilot hole through, and gradually pare back to the marked line.

Rebate the front and back of the carcass members to 20mm, $^{25}/_{32}$ in width by 5mm, $^{13}/_{64}$ in depth, to accommodate the doors and back panel.

Dry fit together before preparing to glue up. Hindsight is a wonderful thing, and I always pledge that in future I will be better prepared for gluing up; however, due note has been taken of Andrew Skelton's useful mitre clamping blocks in the article referred to above.

With its longer open time, Cascamite gives the best chance of a successful glue-up. Check the diagonals and leave overnight to set.

The plinth is joined with through dovetails in sympathy with the rest of the construction, and attached to the carcass with screws inserted through slots to allow for wood movement.

Drawers

As stated, the drawer fronts are of 20mm, $^{25}/_{32}$ in oak, with sides and backs of 15mm, $^{19}/_{32}$ in oak with through dovetails. I find it ➤

"There appears to be some dissension among advocates of the tails or pins first schools"

LEFT: Through dovetails for the plinth, which is then slot-screwed to the carcass

RIGHT: Door panels were fielded and raised using a spindle moulder – an inverted router will also do the job

pleasantly relaxing hand-cutting dovetails, always striving to achieve a better fit.

Regarding the cutting of dovetails, there appears to be some dissension among advocates of the tails or pins first schools; this said I am happier cutting the tails first, then marking the pins from them.

I bought, and was disappointed with, a branded marking knife, but find a cheap utility tool with snap-off blades works well for this.

Marking is made easier because, in order to accommodate comfortably CDs and cassettes, the drawers are all of the same dimension. The sides are strong enough to

groove for drawer linings, so obviating the need for drawer slips, but remember to groove the drawer front's inner face as well.

Cedar of Lebanon (*Cedrus libani*), with its pungent aroma, is ideal for the drawer bottoms.

Drawer assembly

Ensure the drawers are in square and assemble with PVA. Books say that clamps are unnecessary, but that theory depends upon the dovetails, so here is the chance to find out if the pundits are correct!

For drawer runners and record deck slide, *see drawing*; the sliding shelf is jointed and cut just shy of the internal measurements, and mitred on the front edge to accommodate the pull bar which also hides the slides.

The sliding dovetail construction reduces warping of the slide and allows movement.

Frame, panel doors

Again the frames are made from 20mm, $^{25}/_{32}$ in prepared stock. Trim to size and mark out the mortises; I cut these with a router. The tenon shoulders are

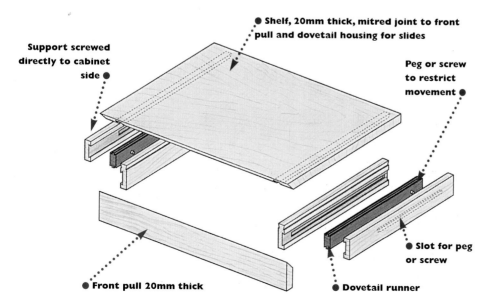

● Shelf, 20mm thick, mitred joint to front pull and dovetail housing for slides

Support screwed directly to cabinet side ●

Peg or screw to restrict movement ●

● Slot for peg or screw

● Front pull 20mm thick

● Dovetail runner

RIGHT: The proportions of the cabinet
are reminiscent of Heals, as are the
panelled doors

ABOVE: Through dovetails again
for the drawers

cut by hand, and the cheeks
finished on a bandsaw. The bridle
joints are cut on a table saw with
the aid of a simple jig.

Mark and cut the grooves for
the panels, again employing the
router, fit the frame together and
measure for the muntins, cutting
the halving joints by hand.

Measuring up for the panels,
2mm, $^5/_{64}$ in is allowed for
movement. With the spindle
moulder, and using a jig for
safety, field the panels on both
sides to allow for full thickness
panels, create the tongue and
improve the appearance. The
smaller top panels are trimmed
by hand.

With an inversion table and a
large panel-raising cutter –
running at slow speed – the
router could be used for this task,
taking progressive cuts for safety.

Glue and cramp the doors,
taking care that glue does not
seep into the panel groove;
applying a little wax to the
panels' corners helps prevent
bonding. After 10 minutes,
ensure free movement and break
any contact with the glue by
giving each panel a wiggle. ➤

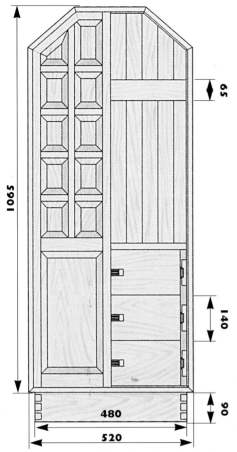

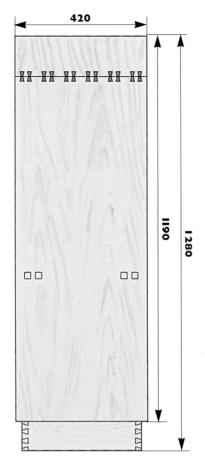

65

140

90

1065

480

520

420

1190

1280

"After 10 minutes ensure free movement and break any contact with the glue giving each panel a wiggle"

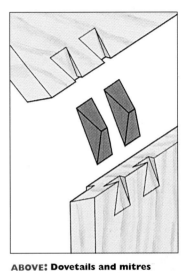

ABOVE: Dovetails and mitres

Clean up when dry and cut the 5mm, $^{13}/_{64}$ in rebate on the doors. Fasten them into place with 3 50mm, 2in brass butt hinges. If available, cranked hinges are an even better choice.

Drawers, shelves

For fitting of drawers and sliding shelf, *see panel*; the slide supports are screwed directly to the carcass side; slotted holes allow for movement. The handles are laminated from sycamore (*Acer pseudoplatanus*) and oak, trimmed to fit recesses cut on the table saw.

For the back panel, tongue and groove 10mm, $^3/_8$ in timber in 50mm, 2in wide strips, and fix into the rebate, holding in place with suitable moulding. Cut ventilation holes to suit the equipment to be installed.

Finishing

All that remains is to fill the decorative dovetails with filler, cutting back when dry with a sharp chisel. Finish the cabinet with garnet paper, working through the grades to 320 grit.

Danish oil works extremely well with oak, and I applied six coats, rubbing down between each application to achieve a pleasant semi-gloss.

EXTENSION RUNNERS

TO ALLOW FOR full access to the drawers, and for the record deck shelf to be fully withdrawn, these components slide on dovetail runners.

The principle is simple; a dovetail housing is cut into the drawer side or shelf bearer, another being cut into a runner which is fixed to the carcass. Between these components is a floating slide, dovetailed on both faces, a small step being left as a bearing surface.

Pegs or screws are fitted to the slide, running in stopped grooves to prevent the assembly from coming apart. The position of these pegs determines the extent to which the slide can protrude: about three-eighths of the slide's length on each face should remain supported in the housing, allowing an overall extension of one and a quarter times the slide's length.

The dovetails are best cut

ABOVE: Dovetail slide allows full extension

using a suitable cutter mounted in an inverted router and guided by a fence. Cut the female part first, then make the male slightly oversize. Trim this to fit the female part by moving the router table's fence a little at a time, until a fit is achieved which is free-running but not sloppy. Apply plenty of wax to the slide before assembly.

Orient-inspired American cherry china display cabinet

Art Deco meets the Orient

Colin Eden-Eadon looks to the East for the design of this airy display cabinet

BELIEVE it or not, the inspiration for this piece – designed to be compatible with Art Deco walnut pieces – came from an 18th century Chippendale cabinet made in the Chinese style.

My client needed a piece of furniture in which to display a collection of decorative Royal Doulton ceramics. A search for an Art Deco cabinet with neither heavy doors nor a dark interior, both of which would obscure the delicate proportions and colour of his china collection, had been unsuccessful.

So, abandoning the idea of finding anything suitable, he decided to have one made. Looking through his library of reference books on antiques, he came upon a Chippendale cabinet possessing appealingly clean oriental lines and symmetry not too far removed from Art Deco ideas.

He also preferred the proportion of a cabinet on a stand rather than a solid, heavy, ➤

RIGHT: Scale model helps the client to visualise the pieces, and the maker to derive measurements

● PHOTOGRAPHY BY MICHAEL MANNI PHOTOGRAPHIC

"I used stopped housing joints and twin-wedged through tenons at the beginning and end of each housing to join the top and bottom to the sides but slotted dovetails could also be considered"

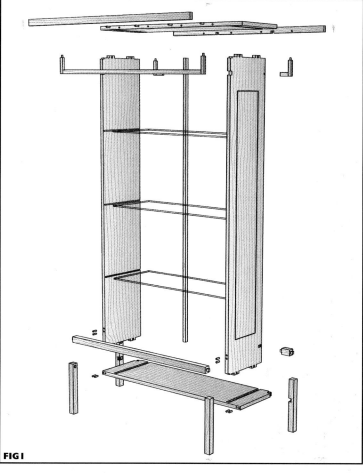

FIG I

ABOVE: Wooden sash bar router fence for skinflints

one-piece design.

The body and legs of my cabinet are made of American cherry (*Prunus serotina*), chosen for its warmth and finely grained figure and to complement the existing furniture; the inlay and feet details are in ebonised sycamore (*Acer pseudoplatanus*).

Scale model

In the quest to come up with an open construction, several small models were made before the final half-scale model in pine and MDF, and it was decided that glass shelves would retain the visual lightness of the cabinet.

The unusual design gave rise to some interesting construction problems. The fact that the cabinet has no back or doors could have resulted in side-to-side movement; its height was also a possible cause for concern.

The problem of how structurally to stiffen the main carcass was solved by tying in the front leg frame to the body of the piece. This action also reinforced the idea of a cabinet on a stand.

The unusual design of the piece dictated the use of a combination of modern and traditional joints, *see fig 1*. The unconventional method of using metal threaded rod as a form of dowel solved the difficulty of how to tie in the front legs and rail.

Construction

Select the best boards for the sides as these will be seen the most and because inlay works to the best effect if it frames a finely figured board. Machine and dimension the boards, being careful to thickness from both sides to avoid any distortion from internal stresses.

Put the boards into stick when not working them so that they are evenly exposed to the workshop atmosphere. Butt or biscuit-joint the boards, and glue up the side panels and top and bottom pieces.

I used stopped housing joints and twin-wedged through tenons at the beginning and end of each housing to join the top and bottom to the sides, but slotted dovetails could also be considered.

Mark out the length of the main carcass pieces and cut to size. Mark out the housing joints and set up a fence to rout them.

For an all-in-one clamping and routing method try placing a wooden sash cramp on its side to provide a straight fence against which to rout.

This also avoids the problem of G cramps getting in the way of the router, finding a straight edge long enough to reach the back of the bench – and then a block to support it – and another G cramp! Paramo sash cramp heads work well as they do not pivot or move around, *see panel*.

Cut the mortises and tenons, rout the housings, cut wedges and dry fit all joints.

Inlay

Before the carcass can be glued up the inlay grooves must be cut with a 1.5mm ($^1/_{16}$in) router cutter, the long grooves with the router's side fence and the short ones by using a straight edge. Placement of a stop will prevent the grooves from over-running. These should be at 2 or 3mm ($^5/_{64}$ to $^1/_8$in) deep and the inlay 5mm ($^{13}/_{64}$in).

Clean the corners out with a fine chisel. I have one which I specially ground for this purpose, *see also David Savage's First Principles in F & C No. 2.*

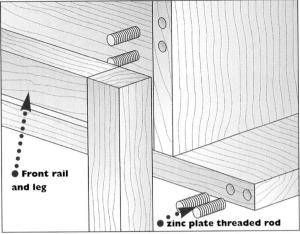

Front rail and leg

zinc plate threaded rod

ABOVE: Fig 2a The metal rod fits into a sleeve of epoxy resin

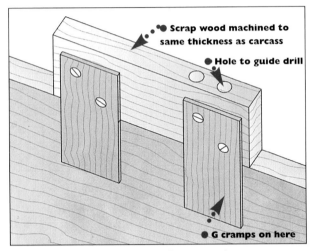

Scrap wood machined to same thickness as carcass

Hole to guide drill

G cramps on here

BELOW: Fig 2b Plywood cheeks allow accurate positioning of the jig

The inlay on this piece is raised and rounded. It may be cut by either following the technique laid out by Frank Rainer, *see F&C No. 4*, or cut oversize on a bandsaw and fitted with a block plane and scraper.

Rounding the inlay can be accomplished either freehand, again with a block plane, or with a specially made cutter in a scratchstock; this latter method will achieve more consistent results but involves more time setting up.

For both these operations a groove will need to be cut in a scrap piece of wood so that the inlay can be held while it is worked.

Because the inlay is raised rather than flush it is more vulnerable, so mask off the groove to protect it during the next stages; leave fitting the inlay until all the rest of the carcass is complete and the legs and rails are ready to be attached.

Shelves

The shelves are of 6mm ($\frac{1}{4}$in) toughened glass, so all that needs doing here is to rout the grooves to accept them. These need to be a little oversize at 6.5mm (a generous $\frac{1}{4}$in) to allow them to slide in easily. Because the shelves are not attached, the sides could theoretically bow out; fortunately, however, this problem has not occurred.

The inside surfaces must be finished and polished prior to assembly of the carcass; glue up using cauls and long sash cramps, checking diagonals for square.

Leg frames

The joints used for the front and back legs and rails are conventional mortise and tenons with secret haunches. For accuracy and economy of time mark out and cut the two joint pairs together.

Once fitted, the joints which attach the back legs to the bottom of the main carcass need to be cut. These are small tenons with a sliding housing cut into the leg, *see fig 3*.

The back pair of rails are then twin stub-tenoned into the side of the carcass.

Front leg assembly

The front rail and legs are now ready to be attached to the carcass. These are pinned in two

places using the metal dowel technique outlined above, *also see panel*. The unconventional construction requires a combination of drilling with a pillar drill and some freehand drilling, for which a jig must be made.

The dowel jig should be constructed of material the same thickness as the carcass and ➤

ABOVE: Front rail assembly

BELOW: Back leg asembly

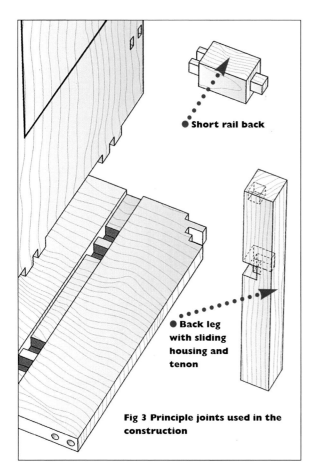

● **Short rail back**

● **Back leg with sliding housing and tenon**

Fig 3 Principle joints used in the construction

ABOVE: Top corner detail

about 100mm (4in) in depth, so have the drill at 90° to the carcass when this stage is reached.

Mark out the position of holes in relation to the thickness of the legs; these must be accomplished on a pillar drill as the jig will also be used to make corresponding holes in the carcass. Once drilled the jig can be used to mark out the holes for the legs; these can then be achieved with the pillar drill.

Pieces of ply screwed to the jig assist alignment and keep it vertical, *see fig 2a&b;* they will also provide an area on which the jig can be clamped to the carcass.

The corresponding holes in the carcass can now be drilled. This part of the leg assembly is very critical and requires a clear head! The thickness of material being worked with is not great, so when the holes for the dowels are being drilled into the carcass accuracy is paramount.

Providing the jig is set up properly all should be well. The diameter of the threaded rod for this piece is 8mm ($^5/_{16}$in).

Top assembly

The top assembly is more easily cut and fitted before the leg and rails are assembled and glued up,

otherwise the whole becomes too cumbersome to secure on the bench.

The only joint involved in the construction of the top is a small housing on each of the sides for the top rail. The top, front and back 'cornice' pieces and the decorative squares are simply dowelled together; the dowel can either be wooden or metal. Once it is all fitted it can be glued up.

Finishing

The inlay can now be fitted, mitred and glued in. The ebonised sycamore feet are doweled on before the final glue-up of the legs and rails.

I used Danish oil throughout the cabinet, inside and out. Each coat was brushed on and left for no longer than 10 minutes before being wiped off with a cloth.

I would suggest a minimum of three coats, leaving each coat to dry fully before applying the next.

The unusual aspects of this cabinet made it interesting to make. The customer feels that the finished piece achieves exactly the balance he was seeking for his collection and its surroundings, and it has even received some favourable comments from non Art Deco enthusiasts.

"This part of the leg assembly is very critical and requires a clear head"

Sweet chestnut

Andrew Lawton makes an Arts and Crafts-influenced dressing table and mirrors on a limited budget

PHOTOGRAPHY BY STEPHEN HEPWORTH, MAIN ILLUSTRATION BY IAN HALL

● **ANDREW LAWTON**, a member of the Society of Designer Craftsmen, has been making furniture full-time since 1980. He rescued Goatscliffe Workshops – run by pioneer craftsman Ben Coopland from the 1920s to 1960s – in Grindleford, Derbyshire from near dereliction. Lawton's 1991 Spiral Table in English walnut inlaid with sycamore received a Guild Mark from the Worshipful Company of Furniture Makers.

ALL PROFESSIONAL cabinetmakers enjoy making speculative pieces for exhibitions as these give them the opportunity to realise ideas which have been forming in their heads and appearing in their sketchbooks.

Similarly welcome are clients who are willing and able to pay for the extra hours involved in adding refinements such as inlays or intricate veneering, always provided that such embellishments are appropriate and not just a display of the client's wealth or the maker's skill.

In many workshops though – certainly in mine – such circumstances are the exception. Much of our work involves making furniture for discerning people of more or less average means for whom paying much more than that asked for the very best work available in the shops is not an option.

The challenge of making a piece within a tight budget is worth accepting in my view; in its own way it can be as satisfying as the no-expense-spared commission.

Design brief

The dressing table in sweet chestnut (*Castanea sativa*) is just such a piece. The client already had several items, simply but well made in English oak (*Quercus robur*), which set the theme, but the firm which made them only worked to standard designs and didn't offer one-offs.

Armed with the client's brief, a design was drawn up. The desire was to come up with something which was obviously the work of a craft workshop rather than a small factory, but within a very restricted budget.

The result is an unashamedly Arts and Crafts-influenced piece, quite similar to work Edward Barnsley was doing in the 1920s, which, 70 years on, still looks fresh and pleasing to the eye.

The construction of the carcass is frankly expressed with through dovetails and tenons. The curved centre rail and mirror supports are intended to soften the overall angularity of the piece, as are the pencil-rounded arrises.

The turned walnut knobs were the client's choice.

Construction

Construction followed this workshop's usual practice of roughing out rather more timber than was needed so as to allow for any components which might move and become unsuitable during its 'second seasoning' period of acclimatisation in the workshop to heated conditions.

Care was taken to achieve a good grain match for the carcass top and especially the drawer fronts – *see Anthony Butler's walnut bureau in Q&A, F&C No. 6 for a perfect example of this -*

as far as possible with the material available.

The careful choice of each piece of timber by a sensitive individual is one of the reasons why hand-made furniture is admired; the wood is not merely a raw material which is mechanically processed.

Carcass

The carcass is made by machine planing and thicknessing the

ABOVE: Through tenons visible in the top, showing contrasting walnut wedges

hallenge

ABOVE: Curved support rail tenons should also be wedged for rigidity, although the wedges needn't be contrasting here

LEFT: Edward Barnsley would surely have approved of the interpretation of this dressing table and mirrors

mortises were cut with an Elu MOF96E router, squared off with a chisel and tapered from the outside to allow for wedging.

Likewise the blind mortises, housings for the drawer runners and grooves for the back panel and kick boards were also routed.

Top, drawers

The top is dealt with next, and the various horizontal rails marked out from it.

All the tenons on the drawer rails, curved support rail and kick boards are now cut by hand and fitted up.

At this stage the two drawer carcasses are assembled dry to check that nothing is amiss, especially as far as the subsequent fitting of the drawers is concerned. In particular, attention should be paid to ensuring that front drawer rails are in perfect alignment with the runners and that the carcasses are parallel in their widths.

A carcass may be fractionally wider at the back than the front but never the other way round; this would guarantee sloppily fitting drawers no matter how well made they are.

To take account of the fact that changes in humidity cause timber to swell and shrink across its width but not in its length, the runners should be put into their housings without glue apart from the front 25mm (1in) or so and slot-screwed or left dry at the back bottom rail mortises, depending on their position.

Drawer runners ought always to be of a hard-wearing timber such as oak or beech (*Fagus sp*), incidentally.

An allowance of 3 or 4mm ($^1/_8$in) must be made in the length ➤

various boards and gluing them up to form the four sides and the top. Normally in this workshop all butt joints have a stopped groove routed along their length and a ply tongue glued in, but on this occasion a biscuit jointer was borrowed from a friend.

Its use certainly saved time – although as a percentage of the total, not very much – but whether biscuits are as strong is debatable. While the biscuits provided ample strength for this job, possibly they would not if used for a large table top or anything subject to strain or very heavy use. (*Actually I've used thousands and they are indestructible in an edge-to-edge joint – Editor*)

After truing and squaring up, all four ends are marked out together, the knife lines carried round, and the mortises, housings and grooves marked. The

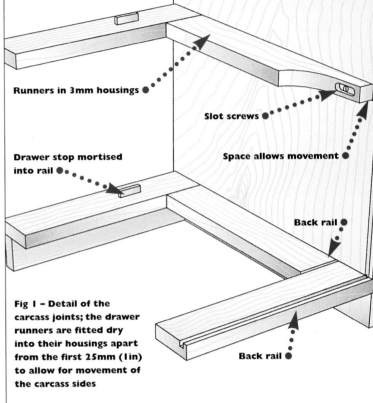

Fig 1 – Detail of the carcass joints; the drawer runners are fitted dry into their housings apart from the first 25mm (1 in) to allow for movement of the carcass sides

Labels in Fig 1:
- Runners in 3mm housings
- Slot screws
- Drawer stop mortised into rail
- Space allows movement
- Back rail
- Back rail

"A few plane strokes too many can make all the difference between a perfect fit and a poor one"

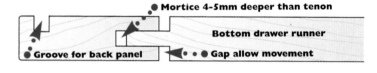

Fig 2 – Section through back rail joint, showing allowance in tenon shoulders to allow for movement

Labels in Fig 2:
- Mortice 4-5mm deeper than tenon
- Bottom drawer runner
- Groove for back panel
- Gap allow movement

ABOVE: With the carcass assembled, drawer sides can be adjusted to fit their openings

of the runners to accommodate any shrinkage which may occur in the future life of the piece, *see illustration.*

Surface preparation

ART OF DOVETAILING

THE DECISION on the number of tails and pins should be based on the appearance desired, in this case neither crowded nor sparse.

I believe there are formulae for spacing dovetails, but I was taught to go for what looks right, and this varies from job to job. The art of dovetailing has been excellently covered elsewhere so it doesn't need repeating here, suffice to say that in this workshop they are always cut by hand, never with a router or any of the weird and wonderful gadgets now on the market.

Even if the job may take a little longer, the sheer satisfaction of cutting dovetails by hand makes it worthwhile, even for the professional maker.

ABOVE: Sawing dovetail pins

ABOVE: Marking out dovetail pins with a knife

The next task is to mark out and cut the dovetails, which have been left until now to minimise any damage to the delicate pins during other operations. A simple workshop-made template may be used to set out the slope which should be 1 in 7 or 1 in 8, *see panel.*

In readiness for the several glue-ups, all internal surfaces are then sanded and waxed, Sellotape being used to mask off glue-receiving areas. Waxing and polishing the interior of a drawer carcass is easier before assembly than after.

The two drawer carcasses are glued up first, with the tenons wedged as previously described, *see F&C No. 2.* Then fix the intermediate runners in place.

The sides are checked in several places with a straight-edge; bowing would affect the fit of the drawers.

Stiffening rail

Kneehole dressing tables and desks of this type can suffer from a tendency to flex and distort,

particularly when being carried. To prevent this from happening, a deep stiffening rail, grooved to take a back panel, is dovetailed to the two bases.

This is fitted after the bases are linked together with the long drawer rail and curved support rail. The latter should also be fox-wedged for rigidity, *see photo.* Since they are purely structural and not normally seen, these wedges need not be of walnut (*Juglans sp*) as on this job.

On work with a more generous budget, framed and panelled chestnut or even cedar of Lebanon (*Cedrus libani*) backs are made, but on this piece 6mm oak-faced ply panels were fitted in grooves.

Have an assistant on hand when the top is glued onto the rest of the carcass; the glue should be spread on the pins of the dovetails quickly and evenly, and the joints driven down as far as possible with a heavy hammer

> **"Waxing and polishing the interior of a drawer carcass is easier before assembly than after"**

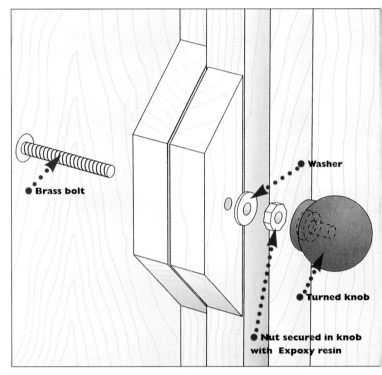

Brass bolt • Washer • Turned knob • Nut secured in knob with Expoxy resin

RIGHT: Fig 3 – Detail of the mirror frame hinge

and stout block of wood, before being pulled home with sash cramps.

The use of a hammer and chunk of wood to spread the pressure sounds primitive but if too long is spent assembling a long row of dovetails the glue can start to grab, exerting a tremendous force which makes hard work of pulling the shoulders up tight.

Mirrors

After checking for squareness the carcass can be put to one side ready for a final clean up, and attention given to the mirrors. These are made exactly as for a light cabinet door, with blind tenons, long and short shoulders and a rebate to take the mirrors. After assembly and cleaning up a second rebate is routed on the back faces to allow the backing panels to be fitted.

To permit the central mirror to tilt, pivots are made from 6mm (¼in) diameter bolts, the nuts being secured with epoxy resin in turned walnut knobs. Tightening the knobs locks the frame in any desired position.

The outer mirrors are attached with solid drawn brass butt hinges in the same way as a door would be hung. The ply backing panels are temporarily fitted; the mirrors themselves are left out until the whole piece has been lacquered.

Oak slips

With the carcass and mirror assembly more or less complete, it is possible to concentrate entirely on the drawers, which have chestnut sides and backs, oak slips and cedar of Lebanon bottoms.

This commission's dividing line between profit and loss being pretty close, decisions had to be taken as to what was essential and what was merely desirable.

For this reason dust panels between the drawers were omitted, but dovetailing the drawers was seen as important, as was the use of oak slips to give a wide, hard-wearing running surface.

Similarly, spending valuable time hand-planing and sanding to perfection the undersides of the drawer bottoms, as one would on an exhibition piece, was out – enough that they were of cedar at all!

There isn't space in this article to go into every detail of how to make and fit a good drawer, but two points are worth mentioning. Firstly, the interior of the carcass should be tested again for any misalignment of runners and high spots on the sides or guides, and corrected if necessary.

Secondly, methodical and unhurried work is important when fitting drawers, when a few plane strokes too many can make all the difference between a perfect fit and a poor one.

Many cabinetmakers rely on small pieces of ply pinned and glued to the rail to form the drawer stops, but a much better way is to mortise the rail and fit a short length of timber end on, *see photo*. These can always be pared back slightly if need be to adjust the position of the drawer fronts.

Finishing

Completion of the piece is now in sight; a thumb-burning going over with a cabinet scraper and sanding with 150 and 180 grit garnet paper is followed by spraying with precatalysed matt lacquer.

Preparing surfaces for finishing can be laborious to the extent that the actual spraying is something of an anti-climax; sanding sealer flatted down, followed by two top coats, steel-woolled between each, a final de-nibbing and the job is done.

All that remains is to fit the mirrors into their frames with small softwood wedges and screw the backing panels on.

The finished dressing table was well received by its new owners, who subsequently ordered a matching stool. Although the table took longer to make than the hours allowed, it was nonetheless an interesting exercise in creating a straightforward, functional piece for everyday use.

SWEET BUT NOT SO CHEAP

TIMBER FOR this commission was a choice between English oak (*Quercus robur*) or sweet chestnut (*Castanea sativa*). At one time sweet chestnut – not to be confused with horse chestnut (*Aesculus hippocastanum*) – was considered to be a cheap substitute for oak, but today the difference in cost isn't that great owing to the relative scarcity of prime chestnut.

It is now seen as a fine timber in its own right, with most of the visual properties of oak, but not the characteristic silver figure or 'flash' of quarter-sawn oak. It is, however, softer – although still much tougher than most softwoods – and more easily and quickly worked, hence its choice in this case.

In tray

Rod Wales on a tray made to complement a pair of boardroom credenzas

● **ALISON AND ROD WALES work together at their Chiddingly, Sussex workshop. Alison studied for a degree in fine art before going to Rycotewood College, then working for John Makepeace. Rod meanwhile went to Rycotewood from Parnham. Since their workshop was established in 1981 they have worked together as designers and makers of contemporary furniture.**

ABOVE: View from the front – note the flare of the sides.

OBJECTS THAT CAN be completed in a day rather than a month or so hardly ever come the way of our workshop, so it occurred to us that this tray could form the basis for a useful project.

The word 'basis' is used advisedly as the design is capable of considerable tweaking, with extra marks being awarded for personal interpretation of proportion, material and detail.

This tray is no more or less than an accessory within a fairly hefty pair of credenzas – can anyone tell me when a sideboard becomes a credenza? – designed for a round boardroom which we recently furnished.

The context for the piece being decidedly on the smart side, more was required of this relatively humble detail than your average beechwood (*Fagus sp*) laminate or pressed metal job – all that is really needed for heaving cups of tea about.

On the other hand, we do not like over-elaboration in a utilitarian object, so our design aims for a degree of refinement without excess.

Optical stretch

The two main features of the tray are the laminated base formed from 1.5mm aeroply veneered on both sides with 1mm English oak (*Quercus robur*), and the long sides which are angled in section and their top edge curved, causing their plan view also to appear curved.

This is an optical illusion, but one which lends the composition a satisfying tension, giving the whole structure a stretched look.

The tray base can be produced most easily by use of a vacuum press. The former – or mould – need only be a sufficiently thick piece of MDF – or laminated MDF – with the angles at each end sawn and planed.

In the absence of a bag press cramping blocks could be used, but deep throated cramps would be required in order to attain pressure in the middle of the lay-up.

When one or two painstakingly prepared lay-ups have been glued to the former, the wisdom of this procedure is realised!

Vacuum press

When using the vacuum press put the whole lay-up into a plastic bag before placing it onto the former and then into the bag press. When one or two painstakingly prepared lay-ups have been glued to the former, the wisdom of this procedure is realised!

Don't lose sleep because the completed laminate is unnervingly whippy; the frame provides all the stiffness required, and increasing the thickness of the base will serve only to increase overall weight, to no advantage.

West System Epoxy adhesive for laminating provides immense stability and strength; it is expensive compared to conventional glues but distortion problems due to gradual water loss – which can be the curse of laminating – are minimal.

Preparing components

Meanwhile, the frame components may be prepared to size, but leaving the sides over-width provides greater support for the router when grooving.

The lower edge of the side pieces can be angled at the ends before a template for routing the groove to the base is made.

If all this template making seems to be far too much bother

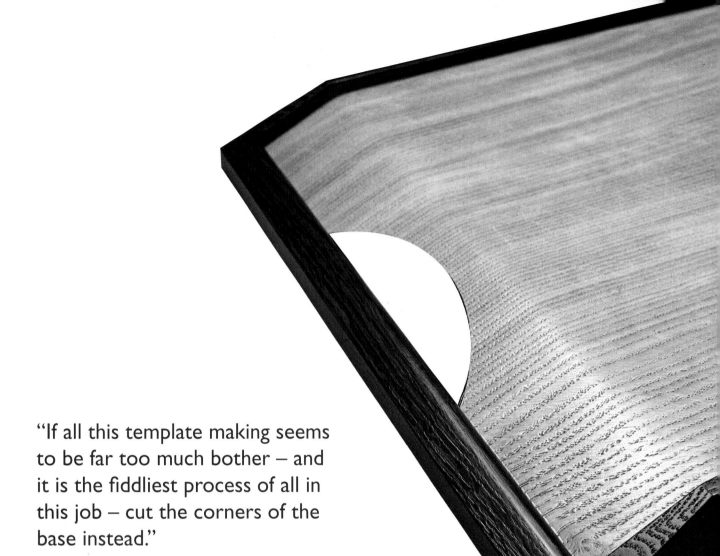

"If all this template making seems to be far too much bother – and it is the fiddliest process of all in this job – cut the corners of the base instead."

– and it is the fiddliest process of all in this job – cut the corners of the base instead.

Cutting corners? Heaven forfend! Should this be rephrased? No: the corners may be cut off, either to make a feature – another dread phrase – with a large void in the corners, or by rebating the corner back by the depth of the groove, thus leaving the corners of the laminate butting up to the sides.

All this means that the groove can be routed from a fence, no template required.

Next, curve the top edge of the sides. This may be done easily by hand, employing a spokeshave,

but in the interests of precision, we also routed this line.

I recommend the use of a template to mark the curve and to aid its cutting out. Use a bandsaw to remove the bulk of the waste.

Handle scoop

The angle on the outside face of the sides can be planed either by hand or by machine with a jig; we use a tilting circular saw to take off most of the waste. The frame ends are prepared by employing techniques already described.

Trim the base lay-up to size

and mark out and cut the handle scoop. This scoop is lipped using a 1.5mm, strip of timber – smaller is fine. Masking tape or Sellotape provides adequate pressure for gluing.

Trim the lipping back with a block plane and sand. The stopped grooves in the ends may now be marked out and routed, the groove ends being stopped well short – about 3 or 4mm – at the handle, and pared back to fit the scoop in the laminate.

Fixing ends

The ends are fixed to the sides by a counter-bored screw which is then pelleted. If other makers feel this method signals the death of craftsmanship, well, bully for them. The not inconsiderable strength of this structure depends on the base being accurately fitted and spot-glued into the grooves.

The frame is designed to be held together primarily by the panel, and is as much a visual and ergonomic entity as a

ABOVE: Frame and handle detail.

CUTTING LIST (finished sizes)

LAMINATED BASE...
by 580 by 335 by 1.5mm plywood one off
580 by 335 by 1mm oak veneer two off

SIDES ....
580 by 44 by 22mm oak two off

ENDS ....
312 by 28 by 22mm bog oak two off

DETAIL AROUND HANDLE HOLE ....
180 by 4 by 1.5mm bog oak

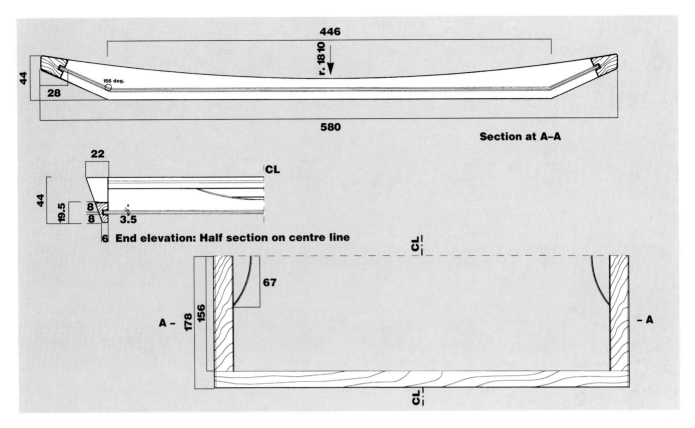

446

r. 1810

44

28

156 deg.

580

Section at A–A

22

CL

44

19.5

8

8

3.5

6 **End elevation: Half section on centre line**

CL

67

A –

178

156

– A

CL

structural one. If readers feel
better using a traditional joint,
then go ahead, have a nice day –
dowels, tenons, even

dovetails in ascending order of
difficulty could be the route to
lasting happiness!

I should add that I'm
talking here about the use of
modern screws designed for
edge-jointing sheet materials like
chipboard and MDF. These
have thinner shanks, and far
deeper and sharper threads
than the wood screws of old that
they have thankfully eclipsed.

Final assembly

When everything is fitted and
flushed the frame is taken
apart, the quadrants and
chamfers routed and final
sanding accomplished.
After reassembly and plugging
the piece was sprayed with a
polyurethane lacquer. For
domestic use a melamine or
even an oil finish would
suffice.

ROUTING THE GROOVES

The template should be
drawn from the trimmed
laminate itself, so
accommodating any slight
spring back at the angled
ends, then marked back
from that line according to
the size of guide bush to be
used.

The difference
between the template
relative to the groove
is calculated by
deducting the diameter of
the cutter from the outside
diameter of the guide bush
and dividing by two. So
using a 3.2mm cutter with a
17mm guide bush, the
calculation is: 17 minus 3.2

gives 13.8, 13.8 divided by
two gives 6.9 – the relative
difference between the
template and the position of
the cut. We used a 3.2mm
cutter for the lay up, the
thick veneer allowing some
leeway for exact fitting by
sanding.

While routing the
grooves, put both of the side
components together on
the bench to extend
support for the router base
and template, and use
cramps and/or double-sided
tape – where would we be
without it? – or even a spot
of hot melt adhesive to hold
everything steady.

Chest on stand

In the first of two parts, **Frank Rainer** describes
how he made a 'masterpiece' for GLOSCAT's
BTEC diploma course

● **FRANK RAINER**
enrolled on
Gloucestershire
College of Arts
and Technology's
first diploma
course in
furniture-making
and design in
1993 after
redundancy from
a senior
management
post. He can be
contacted at his
Silverdeane
Furniture
workshop in
Yorkley,
Gloucestershire
on 01594
562012.

THIS PIECE IS the result of a promise to my wife that I would make her a chest in which to keep items like embroidery silks. The design is influenced by the Cotswolds school, and is based on a stand by Gimson and a dressing table by Peter van der Waals, with handles similar to some by Norman Bucknell.

The body of the chest is in American cherry (*Prunus serotina*) and the stand and inlaid lines are in African padauk (*Pterocarpus soyauxii*). The drawer sides are in maple (*Acer saccharum*) – but quarter-sawn sycamore (*Acer pseudoplatanus*) might have been a better choice as maple is a little unstable.

The stand

Like most tropical hardwoods, padauk has an interlocked grain with a coarse texture that can be difficult to work, so sharp tools are compulsory.

All the stand components are machined to their major dimensions and the legs, top and bottom rails of the end frames marked out for their mortise and tenons, as are the top straight stretcher and the straight mid rails for each end frame.

A single tenon is used for each octagonal leg. The mortises and tenons are cut before any shaping is carried out.

To form the octagonal section on the legs the table saw is canted over to 45°. Each leg is then eased between blade and fence with the help of two push sticks. Having sawn the eight faces on each leg, they are hand-finished using a No. $5^1/2$ smoothing plane.

The moulding

The moulding on the ends of the feet and top rails is cut on the spindle moulder. I had attempted to grind one cutter to produce the bottom part of the mould, and the second to produce the top part, with both cutters mounted at the same time in a Whitehill block to produce the whole moulding in one pass.

Do not do this! The cutters were so large, and overhung the block so much, that one quick spin prompted a change of trousers and a rethink. The solution was found in using one pair of cutters for the first half of the moulding and a second pair, and a second pass, to complete.

Curved stretcher

The curved stretcher is made by machining a piece of padauk to 12mm, $^1/2$in thick. A matching piece of 6mm MDF is marked out to finished size and shape and carefully bandsawed to make a template.

The rough edges are then carefully finished using plane, spokeshaves, sanding discs and blocks.

The finished template is laid on the padauk and drawn around, the padauk then being cut to rough shape on the bandsaw. The template is fixed with double-sided tape to the padauk, which is then trimmed to shape with a bearing-guided cutter in an inverted router. Make sure that you use a template-grade of tape for this operation to avoid slipping.

Mid rails

The mid rails for each end frame are marked out for the double square mortises for the curved stretcher, which are then cut.

The tenons on the curved rail are cut by hand, taking small

RIGHT: Arts and Crafts chest-on-stand in American cherry and padauk.

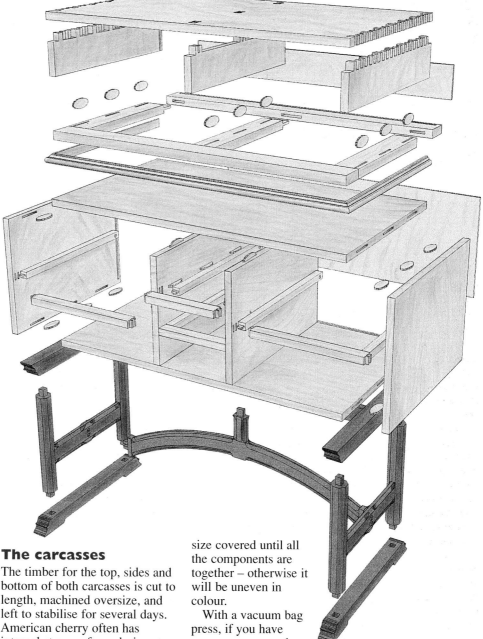

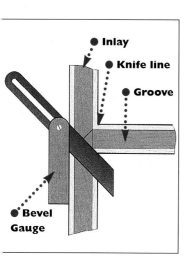

FIG 5 Marking inlay mitres with a sliding bevel

shavings and checking the fit frequently in their mortises.

The munnion

The small munnion between the two stretchers is now made, and the tenons cut; the shoulder which fits to the curved stretcher must be shaped to achieve a tight joint.

The curved stretcher, the munnion and the two mid stretchers in the end frames have shallow stop-chamfers cut with a panel-raising cutter in an inverted router, *see fig 4*.

Gillow's men would have cut these by hand, of course, but I made up a ring fence from birch ply and experimented with scrap timber until I achieved a chamfer which looked right.

The frame can then be assembled dry under clamps to check for fit. If all is well the end frames are glued and cramped first, then when dry they are used to complete the frame, all joints being glued with Cascamite.

Care must be taken in cramping to ensure that all joints are pulled up tight without distortion of the frame.

The carcasses

The timber for the top, sides and bottom of both carcasses is cut to length, machined oversize, and left to stabilise for several days. American cherry often has internal stresses from drying, so it is a good idea to take equal cuts from each side of the board.

The maple for the drawer linings can also be cut oversize at this stage, as the longer this is left to stabilise the better.

Apart from the base of the top carcass, biscuit-jointed, pre-thicknessed boards of cherry are used for the carcasses. I tried to ensure that the figure in both sets of side panels was continuous; this meant that they had to start as two panels, cut to provide the two sets. Care has to be taken when positioning the biscuits to ensure that they are not revealed when the joints are cut.

Because cherry is very light sensitive keep parts at finished size covered until all the components are together – otherwise it will be uneven in colour.

With a vacuum bag press, if you have one, veneer enough 4mm birch ply with cherry veneer to make the backs of both the top and bottom carcasses.

Top carcass

The base of the chest's top carcass is a mortised and tenoned frame to which a moulding is added, the timber for this being first machined to its major dimensions.

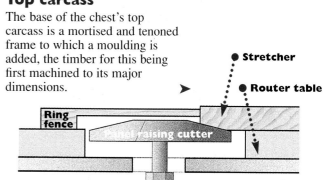

FIG 4 Chamfering the stretcher with a panel-raising cutter in an inverted router.

ABOVE: Base moulding and padauk edge binding on the top carcass.

ABOVE: Base end-frame detail – note the decorative through tenons of the stretcher.

After gluing the moulding to the frame, the profile is cut using radius cutters in a hand-held router, working from a fence.

The side panels are joined to the top with a dovetail and finger joint combination, the centre divider with wedged through tenons. Precise marking out is necessary because all these joints are hand cut. Although I had drawn out the joint spacing on paper, I marked out with a knife the dovetail/finger joint combination on scrap board about six times before achieving exact spacings.

The centre divider is also located in a 3mm, $\frac{1}{8}$in deep housing in the underside of the top; this keeps it straight, so facilitating the free

BELOW: Stand is made from padauk and features revealed construction.

movement of the drawers. The tenons on their own may not stop the panel from warping.

The side and centre panels are joined to the base frame with biscuits.

Each panel is grooved to accept the veneered plywood back. A well-fitting back means that, when gluing up, the squareness of the chest is almost assured.

At this stage I should have put the rebate in the front outside edges of the side and top panels to take their padauk edge binding. I actually forgot, making the operation very much more difficult as I then

had to cut the rebate when the chest had been glued up.

I cut small mortises in the base frame to take drawer stops. They are placed several millimetres further back than necessary so that a shouldered stop can be used, its front face being pared away to adjust the drawer position exactly.

Gluing up

To aid cramping I use bowed blocks made up out of three by two inch softwood, their length being the depth of the chest. Because the face which lies on the chest is curved, cramping at the ends also applies pressure at the centre.

The reasonably long open period allowed by Cascamite at 20°C or less is useful as the dovetail/finger joints take time to coat thinly with glue and then to assemble, as do the wedged tenons.

When the glue has gone off, clean off any residue, wrap the finished top carcass in a blanket and put it out of harm's way.

Main carcass

This is made from solid cherry panels made up as before from boards biscuit jointed together. Again, the two centre dividers have their depth reduced to accommodate a one-piece back panel, let into grooves in the main carcass members.

The drawer rails are jointed to the panels using a mortise and tenon, while unglued biscuits are

ABOVE: **Top carcass features dovetail and finger joint detail at the corners...**

ABOVE: **...and double wedged tenons for the centre divider.**

ABOVE: **Note the radiused padauk inlay to the base carcass.**

"Because cherry is very light sensitive keep parts at finished size covered until all the components are together"

used to fix the runners to the panels, a screw holding them in position at the back and a stub tenon at the front. The joints on the runners are left dry to allow for movement of the solid panels.

Before gluing up, all parts are sanded to 240 grit.

This carcass is joined using biscuits with the back in place, cramps holding the body square. The diagonals must be checked for absolute square – the drawers must fit perfectly.

When the main carcass is dry the padauk inlay can be added to the rails and carcass members. This was done with an 8mm two flute cutter, in a small router fitted with a 12mm guide bush. so that the groove for the inlay could be cut when the chest was assembled.

A length of 18mm MDF, with a planed edge to guide the cutter down the middle of the edge faces of each panel, was positioned on the chest and ➤

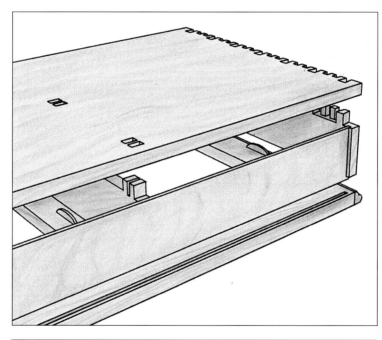

LEFT: **FIG 2 Top carcass rear view – note grooving for back panel.**

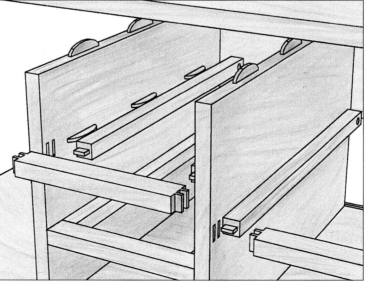

LEFT: **FIG 3 Drawer rails tenoned to side, runners tenoned to rails, dry biscuited to carcass and restrained at back by woodscrew.**

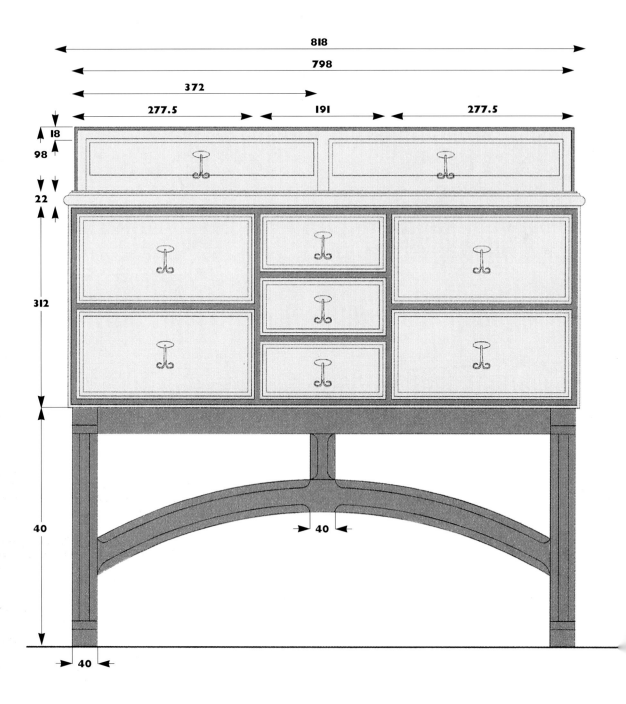

firmly clamped.

The groove was cut to 3mm deep, taking great care at the end of each run – better to under-run than over-run. The corners were cleaned up with a wide chisel.

Fitting the inlay

Now came the tricky part – fitting the inlay. *For how to make it, see panel*. Mine was just too wide by a gnat's thingy to fit, so a couple of light passes with a sharp scraper down the edge gave the required fit.

The mitres are cut by eye using

chisels, a one inch bevel-edged example being perfect for the corner mitres. The flat face of the chisel should be highly polished – this will reflect the inlay when the tool is held perpendicular to it, giving a visual check.

The outside inlays are fitted dry before the inlays on the edge of the two inside panels are fixed.

The mitre socket in these outer inlays is cut by knifing lines with the aid of a mitre square or, in my case, a sliding bevel set at 45°, *see fig 5*, which are then cut with a chisel.

The inlay to be fitted into this socket is cut using the same method, supplemented by some judicious trimming.

The inlays in the drawer rails are fitted in a similar manner, then eased out, glued, pushed back in and cleaned up.

The top and the bottom parts of the chest are now joined together with biscuits, Cascamite and cramps – and the join is invisible! ■

● **Part two of this project, on page 102, concludes with drawers, pulls and finishing.**

454

444

40

50

110

"My inlay was just too wide by a gnat's thingy to fit, so a couple of light passes with a sharp scraper down the edge gave the required fit"

ABOVE: Producing inlay with a table saw

THE INLAY IS made from a padauk board which is slightly longer than the width of the cabinet, 8mm thick by 100mm wide, $^5/_{16}$in thick by 4in. The edges are planed flat and square, then the edge is rounded with a 16mm, $^5/_8$in edge-radius router cutter.

The depth of the inlay is 5mm, $^3/_{16}$in. Remove the riving knife from the saw bench, leaving a fine-toothed blade – 96 teeth on 12in diameter, 80 on 10in, for example – protruding from the table.

Set the distance between fence and blade to exactly 5mm, $^3/_{16}$in. Push a piece of 12mm, $^1/_2$in MDF that is as long as the saw table is deep through the saw until it reaches the back of the saw's bed; stop the saw. Clamp the MDF to the table to prevent the piece that is being cut off from disappearing into the dust chute.

Lower the blade below the level of the MDF. Place the padauk board against the fence but over the blade, and clamp a second piece of MDF, this time 18mm, $^3/_4$in thick, long edge down, to the fence so that the padauk is held down, but is free enough to run.

Remove the padauk and start the saw, raising the blade until the teeth have just sunk into the MDF hold-down, then lower the blade one turn to give clearance for the sawdust while still enclosing the blade.

The padauk is now fed through the blade using a push stick. Check the inlay for correct thickness, adjusting as necessary.

BELOW: Hold-down piece removed.

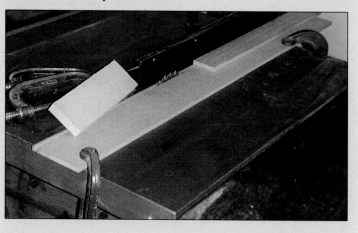

"The vertical position of the handles was only arrived at after much discussion with colleagues"

RIGHT: Chest on stand in cherry and padauk

Chest on stand

In part two, Frank Rainer describes how he completed his college 'masterpiece'

● **FRANK RAINER** enrolled on Gloucestershire College of Arts and Technology's first BTEC diploma course in furniture-making and design in 1993 after redundancy from an insurance company where he had been a senior manager. The piece he describes was made as a design and build project to complete the course. He can be contacted at his Silverdeane Furniture workshop in Yorkley, Gloucestershire on 01594 562012.

THIS SEWING CHEST, used by my wife to store her embroidery silks, is based on a stand by Gimson, a dressing table by Peter van der Waals and handles similar to those by Norman Bucknell.

The body of the chest is in American cherry (*Prunus serotina*), and the stand and inlaid lines are in African padauk (*Pterocarpus soyauxii*). The drawer sides are in hard maple (*Acer saccharum*) — found to be a little unstable; with hindsight I would choose quarter sawn sycamore (*Acer pseudoplatanus*).

The piece is constructed in three parts: the stand; the top part with two drawers and the moulding; and the main body of the chest. All visible joints, including drawer joints, are hand cut. The remainder are machine cut, with either a tenoner or a biscuit jointer.

Part one took the project to its halfway stage, and the following describes the construction of the drawers and trays, together with a guide to lining them with velvet, *see panel*.

Drawer fronts

Because the figure runs through all nine drawer fronts, these must be cut after planing and thicknessing in sequence from the same board.

The fronts are trimmed with a hand plane so that each just pushes into its opening before seizing, with about one-third of its thickness protruding.

Each front must be marked so that its orientation in the opening is noted, together with its position.

To produce the square-edged raised panel on the front face of the drawer fronts a spindle moulder was first set up with a rebating head; a pair of cutters mounted in a Whitehill block were ground to produce the small moulding, but the whole operation could be carried out with a router.

The holes to take the fixing stud of the handles are then drilled in the front face. Central positioning of the horizontal did not pose a problem, but the ideal vertical position was only arrived at after much discussion with colleagues.

The drawer sides and back are cut to exact size and again planed to fit tightly. The backs are sized to push to the rear of their openings with very little play, ensuring that they are rattle-free.

Dovetails and slips

The tails are cut first, and pins marked from these. If taking the trouble to hand cut dovetails then the pins should be made as fine as possible — why end up with dovetails that look as if they were made with a router?

When marking out, bear in mind that the lower pins on the drawer fronts need to be fine enough to allow the groove for the bottom to run through the tail socket. The pin sockets are made to the same depth as the thickness of the sides, erring towards shallow rather than deep to give scope for planing down to fit.

The sides, back and front are glued together with careful cramping to ensure that the drawers are absolutely square with no wind.

The small moulding on the

ABOVE: Hand dovetails should look hand made

ABOVE: Moulding to edge of drawers accomplished on a spindle moulder; a router could be used

ABOVE: Trays slide on maple runners, dry screwed for later removal

"I understand that the measure of a good fit is that, with the drawer two-thirds home, there should be virtually no wobble in either the vertical or horizontal planes"

drawer slips was produced with a scratch stock before cutting the groove for the bottom. If the groove had been cut first, the pressure from the scratch stock on the remaining thin section might have caused problems.

The slips are cut about 1mm over length and the front ends trimmed square on a disc sander. The slips are then glued and cramped in place. The groove in the drawer front should line up perfectly with the groove in the slip.

When dry, the length of the slip is planed flush to the back. Each drawer is then lightly cleaned up to remove any surplus glue.

The drawer slips were fixed after gluing to ensure a perfect fit, but I think now that I should have glued the slips in place first; the bottoms could then have been used to help maintain squareness.

I cheated when making the bottoms, in that they are of birch ply rather than solid timber, but I did veneer both sides of the ply with cedar of Lebanon (*Cedrus libani*). Not only does the appropriate smell waft out when the drawers are opened, but also moths are repelled.

Fitting drawers

Fitting the drawers is demanding. I used my No.3 plane, very sharp and set for a fine cut. Each drawer is offered up to its opening and lightly pushed in until it just binds.

Each high spot is skimmed with the plane, and the drawer offered up again to find the next. This process is repeated until a fit like a piston's is achieved, smooth but with some resistance; if a drawer is pushed home quickly other drawers should pop out owing to the internal air pressure.

The drawer stops, having been glued in, are shaved on their front faces to stop the drawers in exactly the right place.

The top drawers are divided in half, front to back, with a partition. The chest is designed so that the small middle drawers can accommodate trays; the ➤

LINING THE DRAWERS

TWO DIFFERENT methods are used to line the drawers with velvet. For the trays the material is cut into squares, with the corners cut out so that when the fabric is put into the trays and tucked into the corners it folds with no overlap.

Copydex adhesive is applied to the tray only. When the glue is dry, the velvet is trimmed to the tray sides with a sharp pair of scissors and the nap raised with a clothes brush.

For the large drawers, pieces of 270gm card are cut to the same size minus 1mm, $^3/_{64}$in as each side, front, back and bottom of the drawer. The velvet is cut to 20mm, $^3/_4$in larger all round than the card.

Double-sided tape is run in a strip lengthwise down the middle of the card, and the card is placed in the middle of the velvet so that the tape

is stuck to the plain face of the cloth.

Double-sided tape is then run around the outside edge of the card and the velvet turned over onto it, the corners being mitred to effect a stiff velvet sheet.

Starting from the bottom, strips of double-sided tape are run down the undersides of the sheet, the two outside edges and the middle. When this is pushed home in the drawer, it is held firm and flat.

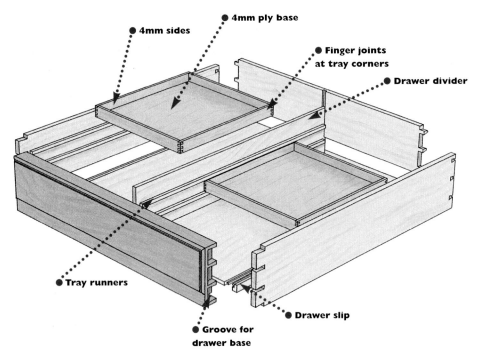

- **4mm sides**
- **4mm ply base**
- **Finger joints at tray corners**
- **Drawer divider**
- **Tray runners**
- **Groove for drawer base**
- **Drawer slip**

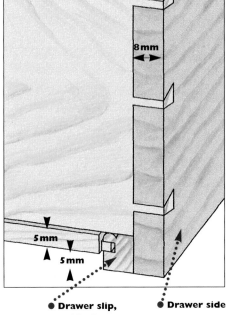

- **8mm**
- **5mm**
- **5mm**
- **Drawer slip, provides larger surface area for running on and enables sides to be made thinner**
- **Drawer side**

"I leave the oil on for five to 10 minutes, which, on a large piece means that it is time to start rubbing off as soon as the last brush stroke is made"

inboard half of the top drawers can take trays of the same size.

There are three trays to each drawer, giving a total of 15, and these are arranged on top of each other on their own runners — providing drawers within drawers.

I had intended to joint the trays with through dovetails, but, as time was running out, my friends at Wealden Tool Company came up with a series of slotting cutters mounted on one arbor that allowed me to cut fine finger joints.

The bottoms, made from 4mm birch ply with rebated sides, are cut to the exact dimensions of the rebated opening. Only light cramping pressure is needed when gluing up.

The tray runners are made from 4mm square maple, screwed dry to the drawer sides, as it is likely that in the future at least one drawer will be required without trays.

Assembly and finish
The padauk takes a good finish even though it has a coarse texture, and the wonderful, fine texture of the cherry gives an excellent result.

I sanded all visible faces and the drawer sides to 320 grit and applied by brush a coat of

Blackfriars Danish Oil.

I have come to the conclusion that Blackfriars must have more solids in it than Rustins as it seems to thicken more quickly after each application, and seems to build more rapidly too.

I leave the oil on for five to 10 minutes which, on a large piece, means that it is time to start rubbing off with a clean lint-free cloth as soon as the last brush stroke is made.

When the first coat is dry, apply a second with 0000 wire wool, so as to denib and smooth the previous coat at the same time as applying the new one. The oil seems to dry much quicker by this method, probably because a much thinner coat is applied.

Continue this process, one panel at a time, until eight coats are applied on external surfaces and three on inner.

Leave the finish for several days before applying a finishing wax such as Colron Finishing Wax, again using 0000 wire wool in the direction of the grain.

This is left for 20 minutes, then rubbed up with an ordinary yellow duster to produce a subtle lustre which turns passers-by into touchers. Fortunately this wax seems to be finger-resistant!

Chestnut dresser

Sound mechanical joints mean that this dresser doesn't rely on glue alone.
Mark Ripley explains

PHOTOGRAPHY BY MANNY CEFAI

● **MARK RIPLEY gained a BA (Hons) degree in Three Dimensional Design at Leicester Poly where he specialised in furniture design and making. For the next 10 years he divided his time between teaching woodwork to handicapped adults and furnituremaking, and for the past six years he has devoted all his time to designing and making furniture. He has a workshop in a converted farm building at South Moreton, south Oxfordshire.**

RIGHT: Dresser in sweet chestnut.

THE DRESSER IS an interesting furniture type for a number of reasons; it offers versatile storage and display options and provides the focal point of a room. For a cabinetmaker it presents an opportunity to practise a wide range of techniques in a single piece of work, which makes up for the hard labour involved.

This example is the last in a series of nine individual pieces, mostly free-standing and sharing common design themes. They now live in the kitchen of a Victorian town house where some original pine (*Pinus sp*) joinery still exists, and the designs take their cue from this.

To allow the dresser to fit into the space available it is deeper than it might otherwise be. At 1200mm, 4ft wide it is also quite narrow for a three-door format. This helps to create a chunky feel, but the same design, carefully reproportioned, could be longer and shallower – consequently more elegant.

Timber choice

The selection of wood for this project is down to personal preference. I chose sweet chestnut (*Castanea sativa*) for its light colour which is reminiscent of stripped pine, to suit the Victorian kitchen setting.

Given the origin of the dresser, I think they work best in native hardwoods. Of these, coarser grained timbers such as oak (*Quercus robur*), ash (*Fraxinus sp*) or elm (*Ulmus sp*) are most appropriate, although a good quality softwood like Parana pine (*Araucaria angustifolia*) could work well.

Preparation

Before embarking on the project I mentally divided the job into three sections of more or less equal amounts of work: preparation of the cutting list; joinery and construction; then fitting up and finishing.

Preparing the timber for a complex cutting list can be a daunting prospect, and I sometimes sub-contract out some of the initial machining.

This doesn't, however, include the critical jointing up, facing off and dimensioning of the wider boards, *see panel*.

To face plane wide boards I use a No. 7 jointer plane working at 45° to the direction of cut, the iron being ground straight; it is tempting to grind a curve on the blade to remove stock more quickly, but this creates more work later on.

The drawer linings should be prepared as early as possible, then put into stick in a dry place.

Construction sequence

The illustrations show the construction of a dresser without base shelves and with only one shelf in each of the top

"Preparing the timber for a complex cutting list can be a daunting prospect, and I sometimes sub-contract out some of the initial machining"

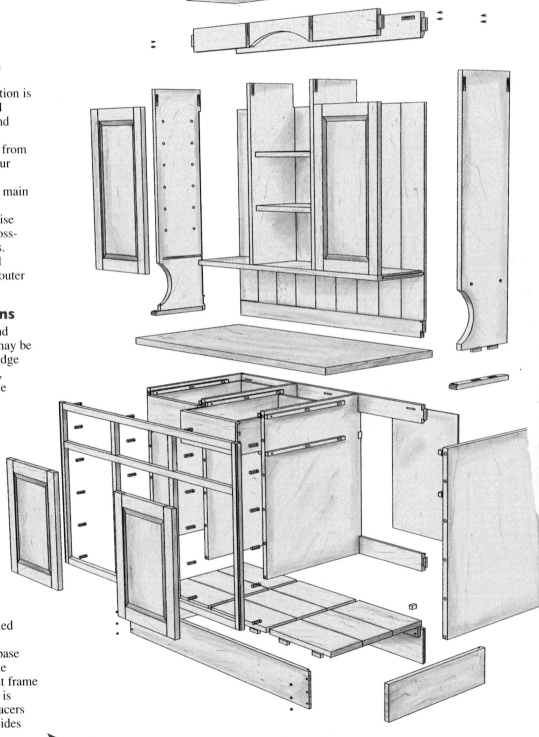

cupboards; these details can easily be altered.

The sequence of construction is as follows: base carcass and plinth; top carcass; backs and bottoms; doors; drawers.

The base carcass is made from a front frame doweled to four vertical panels, with two horizontal rails forming the main structure of the back.

The front frame is a mortise and tenon structure with cross-halvings at the intersections.

A bead is cut into the end stiles of the frame on their outer edge.

Draw pegged tenons

To fit pegs to the mortise and tenons the same approach may be used as in the loose-tenon edge joint, *see panel*. Draw pegs, which pull the tenon into the mortise rather than merely restraining it, are a stronger solution.

Fig 2 shows the relative position of the holes, and the modified peg cut almost to a point to ease it through the staggered holes and out the other side without damaging the wood.

This is worth practising as the positioning of the holes is vital to the success of the joint. The pegs can be made on the lathe or whittled with a knife.

The construction of the base demands a step between the drawer aperture in the front frame and the cabinet sides. This is overcome by fitting ply spacers against which the drawer sides will run. ➤

> "The top carcass appears complex, but with careful planning it can be made in a series of fairly simple follow-through operations"

FIG 3

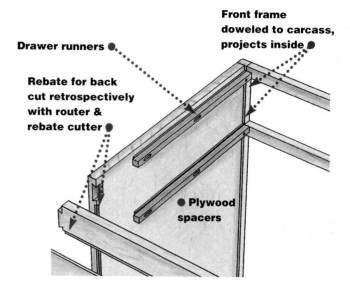

Drawer runners ●

Front frame doweled to carcass, projects inside ●

Rebate for back cut retrospectively with router & rebate cutter ●

● **Plywood spacers**

FIG 2 Draw boring mortise and tenon – 1mm offset between holes.

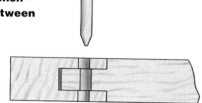

The hardwood top and bottom runners are slot-screwed to the cabinet sides, *see fig 3.*

Base carcass

The construction of the rest of the base carcass is relatively straightforward. The sides and dividers are doweled to the front frame at approximately 100mm, 4in intervals.

The back rails are joined to the sides with lap dovetails, fig 3, and notched and screwed to the central dividers.

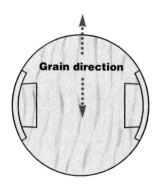

Grain direction

FIG 6 Part section of turned disc showing profile of handle

The small rail to take the dust board above the knee-hole is half-lapped and screwed.

The groove for the dust board must be cut before assembly, along with the mortises for the buttons onto which the top is fitted.

The rebates for the back are cut at this stage, though some of them can be finished off with a rebate cutter and router after assembly.

Ash-veneered ply was used for the cupboard backs and dust board, with solid wood match-boarding for the knee-hole back.

Sand, scrape or plane?

A fine and sensitive finish is produced by the use of a sharp

ABOVE: Handles are turned.

smoothing plane and cabinet scraper, but there is a lot of surface area here. An alternative is a portable belt sander – a difficult tool to use with a consistent degree of accuracy, but useful as part of the process of developing a finished surface.

I use mine as the basis for either a hand-sanded or scraped surface where the grain is wild and does not plane easily.

Once assembled and cleaned up, the plinth is fitted and the bottoms prepared. Keep these loose for now to make finishing less awkward.

Top carcass

The top carcass appears complex, but with careful planning it can

ABOVE: Conventional hand dovetailed construction.

FIG 4 Top carcass detail

FIG 5 Door detail

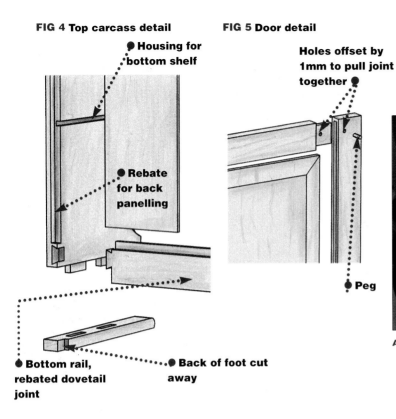

● **Housing for bottom shelf**

● **Rebate for back panelling**

● **Bottom rail, rebated dovetail joint**

● **Back of foot cut away**

Holes offset by 1mm to pull joint together ●

● **Peg**

ABOVE: Drawers are fitted through a front frame.

be made in a series of fairly simple follow-through operations.

Mark out all the joints in the order in which they will be cut, as follows:

● Housing joints – bottom shelf to sides; dividers to bottom shelf; small central shelves;
● Rails – front top rail bridle joints to dividers; back top rail, notched and screwed to dividers;
● Both top rails – mortise and tenons to sides;
● Bottom rail – lap dovetails into sides;
● Sides/feet – mortise and tenons.

When marking out the joints note the arrangement of the feet and bottom rail, *see fig 4*. The housing joints in the bottom shelf are screwed, counter bored and plugged. Once all the joints are marked and double checked they may be cut.

Cut the rebates for the back before assembly. The bottom shelf and dividers are set forward of the ends to allow the back to lie on them, so that rebates need only to be cut in the sides and top/bottom rails, *fig 1*.

The curves in the top rail and sides are cut after the joints but before assembly.

Top assembly

The top may be assembled in a number of stages: dividers and central shelves; top rails and bottom shelf to divider assembly; feet to sides; sides and bottom rail to shelf; then the rail assembly.

To help with cleaning up, fit the housing joints dry and apply masking tape around them, peeling it off when the glue has gone off.

Lastly, make and fit the match-boarded back.   ➤

LEFT: Doors have draw-bored mortise and tenons, back made up as match-boarding.

"THE SIMPLICITY AND efficiency of traditional joinery fascinates me and I find myself increasingly drawn to mechanical constructions, by which I mean structures that work without glue. Glue is used in this design but the piece could work well without it.

Changes in humidity cause wood to move, and joinery has evolved to allow for this. The development of woodworking practice continues and is itself organic – the use of hand planes to cut mouldings, chamfers and other surfaces is both satisfying in operation and sensitive to the material in a way that machines cannot be.

When a piece leaves my workshop I never really feel it is finished. Humidity changes, sunlight and the marks of everyday use are all going to affect the piece, but this is a process which turns a piece of woodwork into an item of furniture with which people will live, and by which they will be subtly affected."

> "I used elm offcuts to make the handles as the grain is very similar to chestnut, with a complementary colour"

Doors, drawers, handles

The door construction is in keeping with the rest of the piece, with fielded panels and draw-bored mortise and tenons, *see fig 5*.

Drawers are of an entirely conventional dovetailed construction; the sides are thick enough at 18mm, ³/₄in to be grooved for the drawer bottoms; drawer slips aren't necessary. Ash veneered ply is used for the bottoms, and the drawer stops are small blocks screwed to the cabinet sides at the backs of the drawers.

The design of the handles, *see fig 6*, picks up the moulded detail from the front frame. A disc is turned to make the profile, the pieces then being sawn, sanded and reassembled.

The pegs are fitted after assembly – I used elm offcuts to make the handles as the grain is very similar to chestnut, with a complementary colour.

Base top and finishing

The top of the base is finished to 28mm, 1¹/₈in. The stock is darker than the rest of the piece and matched the elm handles perfectly – a happy accident.

The hinges are 2¹/₂in solid brass butts, and the catches are double ball, again in brass.

Ronseal Brushing Wax gives a pleasing and durable finish. The main top is finished in polyurethane, burnished and dressed with Danish oil.

To set up the dresser, screw the top section to the base, then fit the base top to the base unit. ▪

JOINT ACTION

THERE ARE VARIOUS schools of thought about improving on the basic glued edge joint. Most of the time a straight and square joint that is glued under pressure is adequate, but, being a little cautious, I like to reinforce it.

Ply tongues increase the gluing area and help to align the pieces in gluing up; however, they are fiddly and time-consuming, and still totally dependent on glue.

I now use a variation of the mortise and loose tenon joint. Mortises are routed into the end of each board – on longer work in the middle as well – and birch ply loose tenons are fitted, see drawing. These are usually about 45 by 19 by 6mm, 1³/₄ by ³/₄ by ¹/₄in. They provide extra gluing area where it is needed, and can be pegged.

Holes for pegs are drilled before assembly; after assembly and planing the hole is rebored to clear out glue and the tenon drilled through.

If the peg is to be visible it can be turned on the lathe in the same material as the rest of the work, cut to a slight taper, glued and hammered home. If there is a face side where the joint is not to be seen, the hole for the peg can be stopped and a fluted dowel fitted from the 'in' side of the panel.

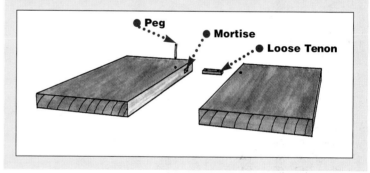

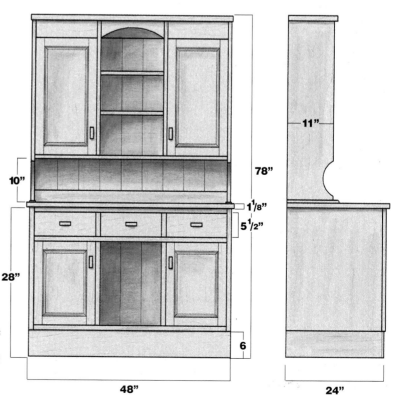

ABOVE: Back legs are morticed for rails on two faces, tenons are shouldered, haunched and mitred

Not a radical design, this oak table from **Paul Richardson** earns its keep as a workhorse

An ordinary table

RIGHT: Drawer kickers are glued to the lower runner

OVER THE last year we have featured many splendid tables as projects: large, small, classical and contemporary, but I can safely say that this one is the most ordinary.

Nothing wrong with that, of course, it will fit in with most styles of interior decoration and in a kitchen can be used as a work surface as well as a four-seater for dining. Many old examples have strange scars running round their edges which correspond with the footprint of a Spong clamp-on mincer; together with the wounds inflicted by children in the throes of homework, these are a testament to their usefulness.

They do, however, dictate the decorative treatment; for example a moulded edge to the table top would interfere with a mincer's clamp and collect dirt, likewise the drawer front is entirely plain.

In fact the turned legs — courtesy of Keith Rowley, *see foreword* — provide more than enough visual interest.

Back legs

Assuming that the legs are already turned, construction is fairly straightforward joinery with a bit of drawer-making thrown in.

First on the list is to mortice the legs. Mark the legs clearly 'front left', 'front right' and so on, and indicate the inside faces. This avoids ending up with two

"Mark the legs clearly — this avoids ending up with two front left legs"

ABOVE & ABOVE RIGHT: Bandsawn dovetails neat enough for everyday drawers — note projection of tails beyond drawer back

LEFT: Dovetailed drawers should go together with a hammer and need no cramps

front left legs, which has been known.

A shoulder at the bottom and a haunch at the top as used here are a good idea, but many old tables of this type just have a top shoulder at this joint and are none the weaker for it. Older versions also make do with a barefaced tenon in a lot of cases. I went the whole hog with shoulders to both cheeks because I find it easier to get exactly the right thickness of tenon this way — if you do take the barefaced option the shoulder must be on the outside of the rail.

The back legs are morticed for rails on both inside faces — the tenons will be mitred here, *see photo*, so make sure the mortices meet fully — I go about 3mm (^{1}/8in) deeper on both to allow clearance for glue.

Front legs

The front legs are morticed for rails on their rear-facing face only — this might seem obvious, but in the white heat of morticing it is easy to get carried away. Their inner faces are morticed for the lower drawer rail; if neatly done there is no need for shoulders top and bottom, just front and back.

The top rail is dovetailed into the top of the front legs, *see panel*.

Rails and runners

The illustration shows the drawer runners tongued into a groove along the top and bottom of the rails — the top groove is also used for the buttons with which the table top is fixed, *see Mover and Shaker, page 14, for details of these*. I used biscuit joints for the runners, in fact; though either method is suitable a biscuit always wins on speed!

Even if using biscuits a groove will be needed in the top of the back rail and the rear of each side rail for the buttons.

Please note that whereas buttons hold down the table top at the rear of the table, the front is screwed through elongated holes in the top runners and top drawer rail. As these need elongated countersinkings to their underside, cut them before the carcass is glued up or spend an hour fiddling around with a chisel later, as I did.

Simple kickers are spot glued to the bottom drawer runners after carcass assembly, giving the drawer something to run against.

Carcass assembly

Glue up the back legs and rail as one sub-assembly, and the front legs and drawer rails as another. Check for square when cramping, and clean out any glue that squeezes into the as yet unused mortices in the back legs.

When these are dry, they can be joined together with the side rails, then runners and kickers added.

Dovetail sacrilege

It's becoming traditional in F&C to say at this point: "as the subject of drawer-making has been covered extensively elsewhere I will not repeat the description…" which — while true — may be a little too brief, so I'll go into a bit more detail about my approach to making 'everyday' drawers.

When initially planing up the timber for the drawer, leave the widths 3mm (^{1}/8in) oversize and place in stick to settle while making the carcass. When the carcass is finished plane the width of the drawer front and sides and cross-cut the front to an exact fit in the opening — this allows for fitting after the drawer is assembled. ➤

"Imagine what happens if an out-of-square bottom is forced into a drawer"

DRAWER RAIL DOVETAIL

Running on offcuts clamped level with the leg, a router can be hand-guided to within a paring of the knifed lines

Note that the back of the rail is flush with the leg

THIS IS ONE of my favourite joints; it looks good, works well and takes little time to make.

First cut the dovetails' shoulders to match those of the lower rails' tenons, then the dovetails themselves — all this can be done on the bandsaw with a steady hand and good marking out.

Next transfer the dovetail shapes to the top of each leg by marking round the tails with a knife, ensuring that the back of the rail is flush with the back of the legs. The sockets can now be roughed out using a router — clamp each leg between two straight offcuts in the vice, carefully lining up the top surfaces to give a good running surface for the router. With care, the router can be guided freehand to within a whisker of the knife-marked lines, *see photo,* after which a quick clean-up with a chisel results in a perfect fit.

BELOW: Bottom is fixed through a slot to the drawer back — note that the countersinking must follow the slot for a true sliding fixing

Mark the thicknesses of the front and sides onto their mating parts, then it's time for some sacrilege — at least in my workshop it is. Having taped the drawer sides together I cut the tails on my bandsaw, making each set of angled cuts first then nibbling back to the gauged line.

This works just as well with eight drawer sides in a stack as it does with two providing that the bandsaw is well set-up and the blade is sharp, and has saved me days of toil over the years. Obviously the finest work requires that tails be sawn by hand, but for everyday dovetails these bandsawn tails are perfectly adequate.

Transfer the tails' shape to the pins with a marking knife, rough out the sockets freehand with a router, *see panel,* then pare to fit with a chisel.

Unless something has gone very wrong, a dovetailed drawer should not need cramping while the glue dries; put a spot of glue on the side of each pin and tail with a wipe of a brush, then gently tap the joint together with a Warrington hammer, *see picture.*

Now this is where I really disagree with received wisdom, which would have us leaving the sides proud to be planed down later. If instead the drawer back and front are cut 1mm over-width and the dovetail sockets cut 0.5mm deeper to compensate, then the pins will be proud instead.

This means that, once the tails are tapped home, the end-grain of the pins can be lightly hammered which spreads the fibres, holding the dovetails tightly down.

Drawer bottom

Note that the tails at the back of the drawer project beyond the pins — this gives more support against the stress of the drawer's contents being shoved against the back in later life. The drawer back also stops level with the top of the bottom, as it were, to allow for the bottom to slide into its grooves, expand or shrink across its sideways-running grain and be fixed up to the back with a screw through a slot, *see photo.*

As these drawer sides are quite thick they can be grooved directly for the bottom.

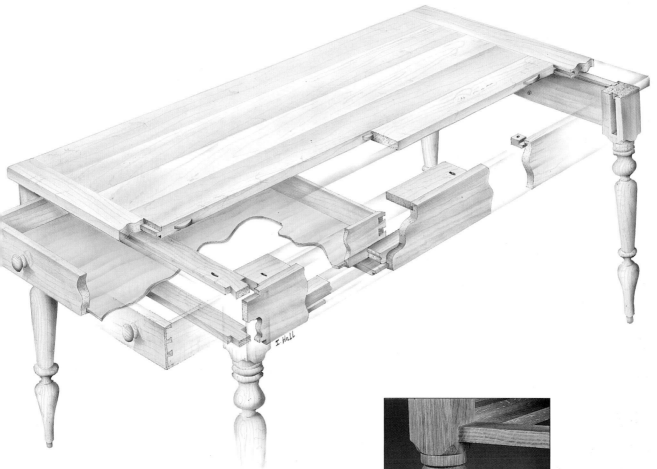

Drawer bottoms are a neglected subject; well made, they confirm the success of the drawer, but badly done can ruin it.

I glue up enough boards of about 9mm ($^3/_8$in) thickness to make the bottom, then trim them to a fraction less than the width required, before cutting the edge that will locate in the drawer front exactly square to the sides — imagine what happens if an out-of-square bottom is forced into a drawer.

Next I run a marking gauge round the edge to give a thickness around 1mm less than the groove, and plane a shallow bevel to meet it, *see photo*. A piece of scrap with the same groove as is cut in the drawer' sides can be run along the bevel to check for fit, but any unevenness will be shown up by the edges of the bevel being out of parallel.

When the bottom fits it can be slid into place, and screw-fixed to the underside of the drawer back through the aforementioned slot.

The drawer is fitted to the carcass, then stops are spot-glued to the back of the runners.

Table top

This is the simplest form of warp-resistant table top possible. The main body is glued up using

"Having taped the drawer sides together I cut the tails on my bandsaw, making each set of angled cuts first then nibbling back to the gauged line"

biscuits for alignment, cut square and a tongue routed at both ends. These are glued, with PVA, into corresponding grooves in breadboard ends, *see photo*.

A more sophisticated version of this is shown in Mover and Shaker, *see page 14,* but this works well and I haven't had one fail yet. PVA allows creep along a joint, and this seems to be enough to allow some movement while not making the joint itself insecure.

As already stated, the top is screw-fixed to the table with buttons at the rear and through slotted holes at the front.

Finishing

I was running a bit late with this project, so for the photography I

LEFT: Nice legs, Mr Rowley

gave it a single coat of Danish oil. Later I'll add a dozen more, cutting back between every other coat, before waxing.

I expect this table to take some wear, so a renewable finish like oil is the safest. ▩

● **Full dimensioned drawings of this table are available to readers of F&C free of charge. Send a stamped, self-addressed A4 envelope to: Ordinary table drawings, F&C, GMC Publications Ltd, 86 High Street, Lewes, BN7 1XN**

INDEX

TITLES AVAILABLE FROM
GMC Publications

BOOKS

WOODWORKING

40 More Woodworking Plans & Projects . . . . *GMC Publications*
Bird Boxes and Feeders for the Garden . . . . *Dave Mackenzie*
Complete Woodfinishing . . . . *Ian Hosker*
Electric Woodwork . . . . *Jeremy Broun*
Furniture & Cabinetmaking Projects . . . . *GMC Publications*
Furniture Projects . . . . *Rod Wales*
Furniture Restoration (Practical Crafts) . . . . *Kevin Jan Bonner*
Furniture Restoration and Repair for Beginners . . . . . *Kevin Jan Bonner*
Green Woodwork . . . . *Mike Abbott*
The Incredible Router . . . . *Jeremy Broun*
Making & Modifying Woodworking Tools . . . . *Jim Kingshott*
Making Chairs and Tables . . . . *GMC Publications*
Making Fine Furniture . . . . *Tom Darby*
Making Little Boxes from Wood . . . . *John Bennett*
Making Shaker Furniture . . . . *Barry Jackson*
Pine Furniture Projects for the Home . . . . *Dave Mackenzie*
Sharpening Pocket Reference Book . . . . *Jim Kingshott*
Sharpening: The Complete Guide . . . . *Jim Kingshott*
Stickmaking: A Complete Course . . . . . . *Andrew Jones & Clive George*
Woodfinishing Handbook (Practical Crafts) . . . . *Ian Hosker*
Woodworking Plans and Projects . . . . *GMC Publications*
The Workshop . . . . *Jim Kingshott*

WOODTURNING

Adventures in Woodturning . . . . *David Springett*
Bert Marsh: Woodturner . . . . *Bert Marsh*
Bill Jones' Notes from the Turning Shop . . . . *Bill Jones*
Bill Jones' Further Notes from the Turning Shop . . . . *Bill Jones*
Colouring Techniques for Woodturners . . . . *Jan Sanders*
Decorative Techniques for Woodturners . . . . *Hilary Bowen*
Essential Tips for Woodturners . . . . *GMC Publications*
Faceplate Turning . . . . *GMC Publications*
Fun at the Lathe . . . . *R.C. Bell*
Illustrated Woodturning Techniques . . . . *John Hunnex*
Intermediate Woodturning Projects . . . . *GMC Publications*
Keith Rowley's Woodturning Projects . . . . *Keith Rowley*
Make Money from Woodturning . . . . *Ann & Bob Phillips*
Multi-Centre Woodturning . . . . *Ray Hopper*
Pleasure and Profit from Woodturning . . . . *Reg Sherwin*
Practical Tips for Turners & Carvers . . . . *GMC Publications*
Practical Tips for Woodturners . . . . *GMC Publications*
Spindle Turning . . . . *GMC Publications*
Turning Miniatures in Wood . . . . *John Sainsbury*
Turning Wooden Toys . . . . *Terry Lawrence*
Understanding Woodturning . . . . *Ann & Bob Phillips*

Useful Techniques for Woodturners . . . . *GMC Publications*
Useful Woodturning Projects . . . . *GMC Publications*
Woodturning: A Foundation Course . . . . *Keith Rowley*
Woodturning: A Source Book of Shapes . . . . *John Hunnex*
Woodturning Jewellery . . . . *Hilary Bowen*
Woodturning Masterclass . . . . *Tony Boase*
Woodturning Techniques . . . . *GMC Publications*
Woodturning Test Reports . . . . *GMC Publications*
Woodturning Wizardry . . . . *David Springett*

WOODCARVING

The Art of the Woodcarver . . . . *GMC Publications*
Carving Birds & Beasts . . . . *GMC Publications*
Carving on Turning . . . . *Chris Pye*
Carving Realistic Birds . . . . *David Tippey*
Decorative Woodcarving . . . . *Jeremy Williams*
Essential Tips for Woodcarvers . . . . *GMC Publications*
Essential Woodcarving Techniques . . . . *Dick Onians*
Lettercarving in Wood: A Practical Course . . . . *Chris Pye*
Practical Tips for Turners & Carvers . . . . *GMC Publications*
Understanding Woodcarving . . . . *GMC Publications*
Useful Techniques for Woodcarvers . . . . *GMC Publications*
Wildfowl Carving - Volume 1 . . . . *Jim Pearce*
Wildfowl Carving - Volume 2 . . . . *Jim Pearce*
The Woodcarvers . . . . *GMC Publications*
Woodcarving: A Complete Course . . . . *Ron Butterfield*
Woodcarving: A Foundation Course . . . . *Zoë Gertner*
Woodcarving for Beginners . . . . *GMC Publications*
Woodcarving Test Reports . . . . *GMC Publications*
Woodcarving Tools, Materials & Equipment . . . . *Chris Pye*

UPHOLSTERY

Seat Weaving (Practical Crafts) . . . . *Ricky Holdstock*
Upholsterer's Pocket Reference Book . . . . *David James*
Upholstery: A Complete Course . . . . *David James*
Upholstery Restoration . . . . *David James*
Upholstery Techniques & Projects . . . . *David James*

TOYMAKING

Designing & Making Wooden Toys . . . . *Terry Kelly*
Fun to Make Wooden Toys & Games . . . . *Jeff & Jennie Loader*
Making Board, Peg & Dice Games . . . . *Jeff & Jennie Loader*
Making Wooden Toys & Games . . . . *Jeff & Jennie Loader*
Restoring Rocking Horses . . . . *Clive Green & Anthony Dew*

Dolls' Houses

Architecture for Dolls' Houses . . . . *Joyce Percival*
Beginners' Guide to the Dolls' House Hobby . . . . *Jean Nisbett*
The Complete Dolls' House Book . . . . *Jean Nisbett*
Dolls' House Bathrooms: Lots of Little Loos . . . . *Patricia King*
Easy to Make Dolls' House Accessories . . . . *Andrea Barham*
Make Your Own Dolls' House Furniture . . . . *Maurice Harper*
Making Dolls' House Furniture . . . . *Patricia King*
Making Georgian Dolls' Houses . . . . *Derek Rowbottom*
Making Miniature Oriental Rugs & Carpets . . . . . *Meik & Ian McNaughton*
Making Period Dolls' House Accessories . . . . *Andrea Barham*
Making Period Dolls' House Furniture . . . . *Derek & Sheila Rowbottom*
Making Tudor Dolls' Houses . . . . *Derek Rowbottom*
Making Unusual Miniatures . . . . *Graham Spalding*
Making Victorian Dolls' House Furniture . . . . *Patricia King*
Miniature Needlepoint Carpets . . . . *Janet Granger*
The Secrets of the Dolls' House Makers . . . . *Jean Nisbett*

The Home

Home Ownership: Buying and Maintaining . . . . *Nicholas Snelling*

Crafts

Celtic Knotwork Designs . . . . *Sheila Sturrock*
Collage from Seeds, Leaves and Flowers . . . . *Joan Carver*
Complete Pyrography . . . . *Stephen Poole*
Creating Knitwear Designs . . . . *Pat Ashforth & Steve Plummer*
Cross Stitch Kitchen Projects . . . . *Janet Granger*
Cross Stitch on Colour . . . . *Sheena Rogers*
Embroidery Tips & Hints . . . . *Harold Hayes*
An Introduction to Crewel Embroidery . . . . *Mave Glenny*
Making Character Bears . . . . *Valerie Tyler*
Making Greetings Cards for Beginners . . . . *Pat Sutherland*
Making Knitwear Fit . . . . *Pat Ashforth & Steve Plummer*
Needlepoint: A Foundation Course . . . . *Sandra Hardy*
Pyrography Handbook (Practical Crafts) . . . . *Stephen Poole*
Tassel Making for Beginners . . . . *Enid Taylor*
Tatting Collage . . . . *Lindsay Rogers*
Temari: A Traditional Japanese Embroidery Technique . . *Margaret Ludlow*

Security for the Householder:
Fitting Locks and Other Devices . . . . *E. Phillips*

VIDEOS

Drop-in and Pinstuffed Seats . . . . *David James*
Stuffover Upholstery . . . . *David James*
Elliptical Turning . . . . *David Springett*
Woodturning Wizardry . . . . *David Springett*
Turning Between Centres: The Basics . . . . *Dennis White*
Turning Bowls . . . . *Dennis White*
Boxes, Goblets and Screw Threads . . . . *Dennis White*
Novelties and Projects . . . . *Dennis White*
Classic Profiles . . . . *Dennis White*

Twists and Advanced Turning . . . . *Dennis White*
Sharpening the Professional Way . . . . *Jim Kingshott*
Sharpening Turning & Carving Tools . . . . *Jim Kingshott*
Bowl Turning . . . . *John Jordan*
Hollow Turning . . . . *John Jordan*
Woodturning: A Foundation Course . . . . *Keith Rowley*
Carving a Figure: The Female Form . . . . *Ray Gonzalez*
The Router: A Beginner's Guide . . . . *Alan Goodsell*
The Scroll Saw: A Beginner's Guide . . . . *John Burke*

MAGAZINES

Woodturning • Woodcarving • The Dolls' House Magazine

Furniture & Cabinetmaking • BusinessMatters

Creative Ideas for the Home • The Router

•

The above represents a full list of all titles currently published or scheduled to be published. All are
available direct from the Publishers or through bookshops, newsagents and specialist retailers. To place an order, or to obtain a
complete catalogue, contact:

GMC Publications,
166 High Street, Lewes, East Sussex BN7 1XU, United Kingdom
Tel: 01273 488005 Fax: 01273 478606

Orders by credit card are accepted